**PRACTICE
MAKES
PERFECT**

Exploring Writing

PRACTICE
MAKES
PERFECT

Exploring Writing

Gary Robert Muschla

New York Chicago San Francisco Lisbon London Madrid Mexico City
Milan New Delhi San Juan Seoul Singapore Sydney Toronto

A version of this book was previously published under the title *Teach Terrific Writing, Grades 4–5*.

1 2 3 4 5 6 7 8 9 10 11 12 13 14 15   QDB/QDB   1 9 8 7 6 5 4 3 2 1 0

ISBN 978-0-07-174715-8
MHID   0-07-174715-X

Library of Congress Control Number: 2010926962

McGraw-Hill books are available at special quantity discounts to use as premiums and sales promotions or for use in corporate training programs. To contact a representative, please e-mail us at bulksales@mcgraw-hill.com.

This book is printed on acid-free paper.

Contents

Part 1
Finding and Developing Ideas for Writing   1

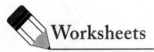 Worksheets

Personally Speaking

Among Friends

School Days

Near and Far

Leisure Time

Recreation

Part 2
Writing the Draft   111

Worksheets

Part 3
Revision

Worksheets

Part 4
Proofreading   175

Worksheets

About This Book

Learning to write is a challenging, multiskilled process. Students must learn how to identify, analyze, and develop ideas. They must learn how to compose sentences, build paragraphs, and express ideas within the standards of written English. They must discover their "voice" and learn how to precisely say what they want with fluency, clarity, and energy.

Practice Makes Perfect: Exploring Writing can be a valuable resource for developing writing skills. It can be used by both students and teachers. Students (working alone or with their parents) can work through the exercises and worksheets to improve their writing, while teachers will find the materials of the book to be useful for classroom instruction or to supplement their writing program.

The teaching exercises and worksheets provide students with meaningful writing assignments and activities. They will learn how to find and focus ideas for writing, how to write a draft, how to revise their writing, and how to proofread their work. This book, which is based on the stages of the writing process, will give students the practice they need to acquire the skills for effective composition and to grow as young writers.

Learning to write is a difficult task. It is my hope that you will find this book useful in that demanding and rewarding challenge.

How to Use This Book

Practice Makes Perfect: Exploring Writing is divided into four parts that concentrate on writing skills, from developing ideas to proofreading. The book includes exercises, worksheets, and an answer key.

Part 1 "Finding and Developing Ideas for Writing" begins with the understanding that solid ideas are the foundation of good writing. Ideas are all around, and you need to learn how to identify and develop ideas for writing. This section includes information on idea development, six exercises, and one hundred reproducible worksheets designed to help you develop material for writing. The worksheets are broken down into seven sections: "Personally Speaking," "Among Friends," "School Days," "Near and Far," "Leisure Time," "Recreation," and "Weird, Strange, and Unbelievable." Each worksheet offers a topic and guidelines you can use to explore and develop the topic.

Part 2 "Writing the Draft" focuses on skills that will help you write clearly. Along with information on the characteristics of good writing, eleven exercises and twenty worksheets address topics such as using proper sentence structure, combining and varying sentences, constructing paragraphs, using active constructions and strong verbs, and choosing a point of view.

Part 3 "Revision" focuses on skills necessary for revision. Two exercises, some "Guidelines for Revision," and twenty-five worksheets are included. Worksheets, which include both fiction and nonfiction, show you the types of weak composition that can slip into your writing. You are required to revise the weaknesses on the worksheets.

Part 4 "Proofreading" examines the skills necessary for proofreading. Three exercises, some "Guidelines for Proofreading," and twenty-five worksheets are included in this section. The worksheets, both fiction and nonfiction, have errors in mechanics. As you find and correct the errors on the worksheets, you will gain skills for proofreading your own work.

Answer Key includes solutions for the worksheets. In cases where answers vary (for example, revision), possible answers are provided.

The worksheets and exercises offer more than 190 separate activities. They provide a rich variety of writing experiences to help you understand the writing process.

Finding and Developing Ideas for Writing

Good writing begins with a good idea. Without an interesting idea, even the most skillful writing will result in a weak piece. At best, the reader will plod through such a piece. At worst, he or she will quickly put the piece aside.

Aware of the importance of ideas, professional authors spend a lot of effort and time identifying, developing, researching, and organizing ideas before they begin writing. They understand that if they start writing with fuzzy, unclear ideas, they will write with little focus or direction.

This is why it is so important that you learn how to discover and develop ideas for writing. Fresh ideas are the raw materials that build the foundation of clear expression.

Discovering Ideas

You have many ideas that can be the foundation of solid writing. But you may not know how to find these ideas. You may not recognize how ideas are interrelated and how an idea can be expanded and refined into new ideas that can become interesting pieces.

To find ideas for writing, you need to realize that you have countless ideas within yourself. Through reflection, imagination, and hard work, you can find much to write about. The starting point is personal experience.

Personal Experience: The Source

The seed of every idea takes root in the rich soil of personal experience. From that seed, the idea grows, branches, and, with the right care and nourishment, blossoms and blooms. Not only our direct experiences, but our dreams, things we hear about or learn, everything that we experience can be the substance of an idea.

The following are some examples of personal experiences that can generate ideas.

- A nightmare can provide the idea for a scary story.
- Seeing a flyer about a lost dog can lead to a story about a missing puppy.
- Learning about the Amazon basin can be the beginning of an essay about the importance of the rain forests.
- Hearing about a big storm can remind a person about a storm he experienced and lead to a narrative about survival.
- A friend's moving away can be the motivation for written reflection about friendship.

Exercise 1.1 Tapping into Personal Experience

Your personal experiences—all the things you have ever done, seen, read, or heard about—can lead to ideas you can use for writing. You must learn how to identify these ideas.

Think about one of the following topics:

- Things That Are Important to Me
- The People in My Life
- Interests and Hobbies
- Things I Like
- Things I Dislike

Now think about examples that can be included under the topic. For example, under "Interests and Hobbies," you might think of reading, skateboarding, soccer, camping, model building, music—obviously, the list can go on and on.

Here are some possibilities how each of the examples can lead to an idea for writing:

- For reading—a review of a favorite book
- For skateboarding—a description of some of the techniques necessary for "extreme" skateboarding
- For camping—a narrative about a fun camping trip

Everyone has personal experiences that can be used to find ideas for writing. Sometimes personal experience can be developed directly into a topic. Sometimes it can be a spark for the imagination to develop other ideas. It is always a source of ideas.

The Value of Keeping a Journal

Writing in a journal is an excellent method to tap into personal experience. In a writing journal, you can express your thoughts and feelings on topics you find meaningful. In time, a journal can become a warehouse of writing ideas.

Writing journals may be a composition book or spiral notebook. Date all entries, because dates provide a time reference that will help you to follow your progress as a writer. Review your journal periodically to find ideas for writing.

Some possible topics for writing in your journal include friendship, home, things I like, happy times, sad times, questions I have, being responsible, hobbies, my family, my pets.

The Value of Reading

Reading is yet another way to tap into personal experience in search of ideas. Reading can present you with new ideas, add information to old ideas, and stimulate reflection on ideas.

The benefits of reading for writing expand your world and experiences. Reading also introduces you to various forms of writing, idea development, and authors' techniques. Virtually all writers are readers.

Seeing Life Through the Eyes of a Writer

Most writers view the world with a sharp eye. They see, they think, and they ask themselves, "What if . . . " To see the world through the eyes of a writer, you should be both an observer and an interpreter of life. Be curious and open to new ideas. Try to step outside yourself and look at things from the view point of others.

Here is an example. Your school is likely to be a familiar place to you. Imagine how it would appear to a new student from another state. What would be the most striking feature about your school? Would the new student feel lost? Out of place? Afraid or anxious? Why might a new student feel this way? Imagine how your school would seem to a new student from another country who does not speak English. Considering situations from another's point of view can help you understand them better. It also can lead to new ideas.

Along with viewing things from different perspectives, always look for details. Use your senses of sight, hearing, touch, taste, and smell. By paying close attention to your surroundings you can sharpen your powers of observation.

Imagine you are standing in your yard or a park. What do you see? Trees? What kinds of trees? Big? Small? Evergreen or deciduous? What about animals? Do you see any birds? What kinds? Maybe you see a gray squirrel scampering along a branch. What do you hear? The rustle of leaves? The songs of birds? The barking of a dog in the distance? What does the air smell like? Clean? Fresh? Full of the scent of flowers? If the day is windy, how does the wind feel against your face?

Against your body? Is it so strong that it pushes you backward? Is the wind cold? Warm? Humid? What about touch? Maybe the ground is soggy beneath your feet because of last night's heavy rain. What about taste? Maybe you are chewing spearmint-flavored gum that makes your mouth feel fresh. Try to experience the world through your senses. This adds to the images that make up ideas.

Exercise 1.2 What Are the Details?

Choose a corner or a part of a room. While sitting, list as many details as you can about this part of the room. Use as many of your senses as possible, though especially sight and hearing. After you are done, write down some of the details you found. Sharp, clear details make ideas come alive.

Seeing through the eyes of a writer broadens the world. It helps you become aware of not just the most important features of things but the smallest details as well. This is a valuable skill for writers.

Focusing Ideas

Once general ideas have been explored, they must be focused. Focusing an idea narrows it down so that the writer can concentrate on a very specific topic. This is important for further development.

Consider the topic "Studying." This is broad and unfocused. Does the topic mean studying in general? Or studying for tests? Or studying a particular subject? The topic does not offer much direction. The topic "How to Study for Math Tests" is focused and serves as a clear guide for writing.

A focused topic provides a writer with direction, and helps a writer to stay on topic. Focused topics are the starting point for clear writing.

Exercise 1.3 Focusing Topics

Think about one of the following general topics:

- Hobbies
- Fun Things
- Pets

These are broad topics that lack focus for writing. Try to find focused examples for them.

Here is an example:

Fun things . . . snowboarding . . . snowboarding at a ski lodge . . . the best snowboarding day of my life.

Note how the topics become more focused.

Here is another example:

Pets . . . dogs and cats . . . dogs . . . beagles . . . my beagle . . . finding Sleuth.

Note how the general topics proceed to a specific one (which refers to the time Sleuth, the beagle, got lost).

These are simple examples, but they will give you practice in how to focus ideas. A focused idea is easier to write about than an unfocused idea.

Developing Ideas

Ideas for writing hardly ever burst into a writer's mind in complete form. In most cases, ideas are discovered and then must be explored, analyzed, and developed. Sometimes an idea gives rise to new ideas that become the focus of writing. Although developing ideas is hard work, there are steps you can take to make the process easier. These steps include identifying relationships, brainstorming, and researching.

One of the best strategies for developing ideas is to consider the five *W*s and *How: Who? What? Where? When? Why? How?* Although each of these questions may not be helpful for every idea, they are useful for most.

Exercise 1.4 Developing Ideas Using the Five *W*s and *How*

Think about how you might build a story from an idea about a lost puppy. Ask yourself the following questions and consider the answers:

- *What?* A puppy got lost.
- *When?* When did he get lost?
- *Where?* Where was he last seen?
- *Who?* Who are the people (and puppy) in this story?
- *Why?* Why did the puppy get lost? Did someone leave the gate of the fenced yard open?
- *How?* How was he found?

Using these questions will help you to expand your idea and build it into a story. The answers to each question lead naturally into more ideas and more questions. The questions serve as a blueprint that will guide you to building a story.

Another strategy for developing ideas is to look for relationships. Nothing exists alone. Everything is connected in some way to something else.

Here is an example. A honeybee visits a flower and takes some of its nectar. The bee returns to the hive, where the nectar is used to make honey. While the bee is on the flower, pollen necessary for plants to reproduce clings to the bee's body. As the bee visits other flowers, some of the pollen rubs off, making the plant's reproduction possible. This relationship helps both honeybees and flowers. Mature flowers are important not only for honeybees. They may serve as food for rabbits or deer, be a hiding place for small animals, or beautify the countryside or someone's garden. Seeing relationships between both living and nonliving things is an important skill.

Relationships can be complex, but basic ones are easy to understand—for example, cause and effect (heavy rains cause floods), interdependence (honeybees and flowers), and parts to wholes (our solar system is a part of the Milky Way galaxy, which is a part of the universe). Learn to look for relationships.

Brainstorming is another strategy you can use to develop ideas for writing. Brainstorming is a mental exercise in which a person writes down as many ideas as he can about a topic. It can be a powerful method in the development of ideas. The purpose of brainstorming is to write as many related ideas about a topic as quickly as possible. Do not pause to analyze ideas during brainstorming, because that only slows the flow of ideas. Evaluation may be done later. Brainstorming is a fast and furious exercise, the sole purpose of which is to expand ideas.

Exercise 1.5 Brainstorming via a Word Web

Creating a *word web* can help you identify, expand, and develop ideas for writing. Write the topic "School Lunchroom" in the middle of a blank paper. (If you wish, choose a topic of your own.)

Think about ideas related to the school lunchroom. You might think of ideas such as the following: noisy, fun, mystery food, recess, seeing friends, talking with friends, not much time to eat, and so on. Write the ideas down. Use a line to connect ideas that stem from other ideas. Write quickly and do not pause to think about ideas now. The goal of brainstorming is to uncover as many related ideas as possible and expand the original idea.

When you are done, review the ideas you write down. Some of the ideas on the word web will probably not be used in writing, but others will. Sometimes a web will lead to an entirely new idea that may then lead to a new web and more new ideas for writing.

Not every writer uses word webs for the development of ideas, but many do. Brainstormed word webs can help you expand ideas into fresh possibilities for writing.

Researching is yet another way you can develop ideas for writing. Along with traditional print sources, the Internet provides writers with resources for finding information on countless topics. Before the development of the Internet, writers often had to conduct hours of research to find information on some topics. Even then, they might not be able to find what they needed. Today, writers often find too much information.

Although the Internet can be helpful for developing writing topics, anyone can post information on the World Wide Web. Not all of the information you will find will be correct or useful. To reduce the chances of finding invalid data, research reputable sites, which include the sites of government agencies, major organizations, and universities. Fortunately, many of the best sites often are listed first when doing a search.

To search for information on the Internet, use key terms. Using key terms directs search engines to sites you will find useful. The terms you would use for looking up information in an encyclopedia or other reference book will result in accurate results with most Internet search engines. Having a focused topic will help you keep on track during research, and can help keep you from finding huge amounts of useless information.

Organizing Ideas

In their enthusiasm to complete their writing, many students take their ideas and want to begin writing immediately. The result is almost always the same: the writers finish pieces that are disorganized. Even worse, the pieces require so much revision that the writers do not know where to start. As a result, they do not do much revision, are unhappy with their work, and become convinced that they are poor writers.

Organization helps you clarify and order ideas and makes writing easier. A basic structure includes an opening, body, and closing.

Exercise 1.6 Basic Organization for Nonfiction

Think about this simple form for structure.

- **Opening:** One or two paragraphs
- **Body:** One, two, three, or more paragraphs
- **Closing:** One paragraph

The opening should introduce the topic and the problem or situation the writing is about. The body, which may be one paragraph, several paragraphs, or several pages long, provides information, examples, and details. The closing includes a final point, or a brief summary of the main ideas expressed in the body.

Find an example of this form in your reading book, social studies book, or science text. It is best to use an article for this activity, as the structure for fiction may not be as clear.

Identify the opening of the article; then the body, including the paragraphs that make it up; and finally, the closing. Most nonfiction follows this format. Look for this form in the articles you read.

Worksheets

The following worksheets are prewriting activities. They can help you to develop basic ideas for writing. The one hundred worksheets are divided into seven sections:

- Personally Speaking
- Among Friends
- School Days
- Near and Far
- Leisure Time
- Recreation
- Weird, Strange, and Unbelievable

The themes of the worksheets in each category are loosely based on the title of the category. For example, the worksheets contained in "Personally Speaking" focus on the author in some way. The worksheets in "Recreation" focus on sports or some type of recreation.

While most of the worksheets are to be developed as articles, narratives, or persuasive pieces, several fiction topics are included throughout the categories. The most fiction appears in the final category, "Weird, Strange, and Unbelievable."

Each worksheet is designed to help you find and develop ideas for writing. Most of the topics tie into personal experiences, making it easier for you to generate material for writing. Because the topics are general, you have much freedom to develop your ideas. For example, with Worksheet 1.4, "The Future Me," you are given the general idea of considering what you might be like in the future. You can pick a time a year from now, a few years from now, or many years from now. Answering the questions on the worksheet will stimulate your imagination and present possibilities for writing. From that point, you can develop the piece in your own way. For example, you may expand the material through brainstorming and word webbing. In some cases, to fully develop your ideas, you may find it helpful to conduct research via print sources or the Internet.

You are to complete the worksheet, using the back of the sheet or an extra sheet of paper if you need more space to answer the questions. After completing the worksheet, expand your ideas and add more details if necessary. Remember that the worksheets are guides. You may find that not all the information you supply in response to the questions on the worksheets will wind up in your writing. Sometimes information not related to the questions will. You may choose a new title that more accurately reflects your writing. Organize your ideas before writing and follow a basic plan of opening, body, and closing.

The purpose of any prewriting activity is to engage your mind with the writing to be done. Once the process is begun, the only limits are your imagination and enthusiasm.

1.1 An Autobiographical Sketch

Directions: An *autobiography* is a true story that a person writes about himself or herself. An *autobiographical sketch* is a short autobiography. Think about your life. Answer the questions and write an autobiographical sketch. Be sure to include an opening, body, and closing in your writing. Support your ideas with details and examples.

1. Briefly describe yourself (age, height, color of eyes, hair, and so on).

I'm 9½ years old, have blue-grey eyes and brown hair.

2. Name three things you like about yourself and why you like them.

The things I like about myself is that I'm good at drawing, I'm friendly and I know how to make friends easily.

3. Name three things you dislike about yourself and why you dislike them.

The three things I dislike about myself are my accent, that I can't smell very well and I don't like most meat.

4. What would you most like to do this year? Why? I'd like to go to Wild Play this year because they have zipwires and you get to climb up 15 meters high.

1.2 My Family

> **Directions:** Some families are big. Some are small. Every family is different from any other. Think about your family and what makes it special. Answer the questions and write an article about your family. Be sure to include an opening, body, and closing in your writing. Support your ideas with details and examples.

1. Who are the members of your family? _____

_____

_____

2. Briefly describe the members of your family. _____

_____

_____

_____

3. Describe some things that make your family special. _____

_____

_____

_____

4. What do you feel is the best thing about your family? Explain.

_____

_____

_____

_____

1.3 Pets and Me

Directions: Think about a pet. (If you do not have a pet, imagine that you can have any pet you wish.) Answer the questions below and write an article about your pet. Remember to include an opening, body, and closing in your writing. Support your ideas with details and examples.

1. What kind of pet do you have? _a notih_ _____

2. Describe how your pet looks. _____

   _____

   _____

3. Describe your pet's favorite place in your home. _____

   _____

   _____

4. Describe how your pet acts. _____

   _____

   _____

5. Describe what your pet likes to do most. _____

   _____

   _____

6. How do you help take care of your pet? _____

   _____

1.4 The Future Me

Directions: Pick a time in the future. The time might be a year from now, a few years from now, or many years from now. Imagine yourself in that time. Answer the questions and write about yourself in the future. Be sure to include an opening, body, and closing in your writing. Support your ideas with details and examples.

1. What is the time of this story? _____

2. Where will you be living in the future? _____

3. Describe yourself in the future. _____

   _____

4. What will you be doing? (For example, will you still be going to school? Will you have a job? What kind?) _____

   _____

5. Describe your family and friends in the future. _____

   _____

   _____

6. What problems might you face in the future? _____

   _____

7. What might you know in the future you do not know now?

   _____

   _____

1.5 Advice for Younger Students

Directions: Imagine that you can offer advice to students who will be in your class next year. Answer the questions and write an article about what they can expect. Be sure to use an opening, body, and closing in your writing. Support your ideas with details and examples.

1. What class are you in now? _____

2. What subjects do you study in this class? _____
_____

3. What materials will new students need to bring to class? _____
_____
_____

4. How can new students be successful in this class? _____
_____
_____

5. What would you like to warn new students about? _____
_____
_____

6. What is the best advice you can give them? _____
_____
_____

1.6 An Important Lesson

Directions: Think of a time you learned an important lesson. Answer the questions and write a narrative about this experience and what you learned. Remember to include an opening, body, and closing in your writing. Support your ideas with details and examples.

1. What is the subject you are writing about? _____

_____

2. When did this happen? _____

3. Where did this happen? _____

4. Who was with you? _____

5. Describe what happened. _____

_____

_____

_____

6. Why did this happen? _____

_____

_____

7. What lesson did you learn? _____

_____

_____

1.7 My Greatest Goal

Directions: Think of your goals. Which one do you want to reach the most? Answer the questions and write an article about your greatest goal. Be sure to include an opening, body, and closing in your writing. Support your ideas with details and examples.

1. What is your greatest goal? _____

_____

_____

_____

2. Why is this your goal? _____

_____

_____

_____

3. What must you do to reach this goal? _____

_____

_____

_____

4. Do you expect to one day reach this goal? Explain. _____

_____

_____

_____

1.8 My Favorite Holiday

Directions: Think about all the holidays you enjoy. Decide which one you like best. Answer the questions and write an article about your favorite holiday. Be sure to include an opening, body, and closing in your writing. Support your ideas with details and examples.

1. What are some holidays you enjoy? _____

_____

_____

2. Which one is your favorite? Why? _____

_____

_____

3. With whom do you celebrate this holiday? _____

_____

_____

4. Describe how you celebrate this holiday. _____

_____

_____

5. If you could make this holiday even better, what would you do?

_____

_____

_____

1.9 My Hero

> **Directions:** Think about a person you consider to be a hero. This person might have lived long ago or might be living now. Answer the questions and write an article about your hero. Be sure to include an opening, body, and closing in your writing. Support your ideas with details and examples.

1. Describe three qualities a hero must have. _____

_____

_____

2. Who is a hero to you? _____

_____

3. Why do you feel this person is a hero? _____

_____

_____

_____

_____

4. Is this person a hero to others? Explain. _____

_____

_____

_____

1.10 Highlights of the Day

Directions: Think about all the things you did yesterday. Did you finish all you wanted to do? Answer the questions and write a narrative about the day that just passed. Be sure to include an opening, body, and closing in your writing. Support your ideas with details and examples.

1. What did you do in the morning? _____

_____

_____

2. What did you do in the afternoon? _____

_____

_____

3. What did you do in the evening? _____

_____

_____

4. What was your most important accomplishment? Explain. _____

_____

_____

5. What did you not finish? Explain. _____

_____

_____

1.11 My Greatest Responsibilities

Directions: Think of your responsibilities. Some of your responsibilities might include doing well in school, watching a younger brother or sister, or taking care of a pet. Answer the questions and write an article about your responsibilities. Be sure to include an opening, body, and closing in your writing. Support your ideas with details and examples.

1. What are some of your responsibilities? _____

   _____

   _____

2. What is your most important responsibility? _____

   _____

   _____

3. Give some examples of how you handle this responsibility. _____

   _____

   _____

4. Why is this responsibility the most important? _____

   _____

   _____

5. How do you feel about this responsibility? _____

   _____

   _____

1.12 An Exciting Event

Directions: Think of a time you took part in or watched an exciting event. Answer the questions and write a narrative about this experience. Be sure to include an opening, body, and closing in your writing. Support your ideas with details and examples.

1. What was the event? _____

2. When did the event take place? _____

3. Where did it take place? _____

4. Who was with you? _____

5. Describe what happened at the event. _____

_____

_____

_____

6. Why was the event exciting? _____

_____

_____

7. What was the best part of the event? _____

_____

_____

_____

1.13 Someone I Admire

Directions: Think about a person you admire. This person might be living, or he or she might have lived in the past. Answer the questions and write an article about this person. Be sure to include an opening, body, and closing in your writing. Support your ideas with details and examples.

1. Who is the person you admire? _____

2. How do you know this person? _____

3. Describe this person. _____

_____

_____

_____

4. What is special about this person? _____

_____

_____

_____

_____

5. Why do you admire this person? _____

_____

_____

_____

1.14 A Special Talent

Directions: Everyone has special talents. Think about what you do better than other people. Answer the questions and write about your special talent. Be sure to include an opening, body, and closing in your writing. Support your ideas with details and examples.

1. What is your special talent? _____

2. What skills or knowledge does this talent require? _____

_____

_____

3. How did you develop this talent? _____

_____

_____

_____

4. What advice could you give others so that they may develop this talent?

_____

_____

_____

5. How might you improve your special talent? _____

_____

_____

_____

1.15 One of the Most Important Things in My Life

Directions: Think about something or someone that is important to you. Answer the questions and write an article about what is important in your life. Be sure to use an opening, body, and closing in your writing. Support your ideas with details and examples.

1. What is most important to you? _____

_____

_____

2. Why is this important? _____

_____

_____

_____

_____

3. What do you do to show that this is important to you? _____

_____

_____

_____

4. How would your life be different if this was not a part of your life?

_____

_____

_____

1.16 What's a Friend?

Directions: Think about your friends. What makes a person a friend? Answer the questions and write an article explaining what you believe a friend is. Be sure to include an opening, body, and closing in your writing. Support your ideas with details and examples.

1. What is one trait of a friend? Give an example of this trait.

_____

_____

_____

2. What is a second trait of a friend? Give an example of this trait.

_____

_____

_____

3. What is a third trait of a friend? Give an example of this trait.

_____

_____

_____

4. What is the most important trait a friend should have? Explain.

_____

_____

_____

Among Friends

1.17 Rules for Getting Along with Others

Directions: Think about people you know who get along well with others. Now think about some people who do not get along with others. Answer the questions; then write an article about rules people should follow to get along with others. Be sure to include an opening, body, and closing in your writing. Support your ideas with details and examples.

1. Write one rule people should follow if they hope to get along with others. Why is this rule important?

   _____

   _____

   _____

2. Write a second rule people should follow if they hope to get along with others. Why is this rule important?

   _____

   _____

   _____

3. Write a third rule people should follow if they hope to get along with others. Why is this rule important?

   _____

   _____

   _____

   _____

1.18 Fun with Friends

Directions: Think of a great time you had with a friend. Maybe you went to a party, a sports event, or an amusement park. Or maybe you just hung out. Answer the questions; then write a narrative about a fun time you had with a friend. Be sure to include an opening, body, and closing in your writing. Support your ideas with details and examples.

1. Who is your friend? _____

2. Where did you go? _____

3. When did you go? _____

4. Who else was present? _____

_____

5. How did you get there? _____

_____

6. Describe this fun time. What did you do? _____

_____

_____

7. Why was this time so much fun? _____

_____

_____

_____

Among Friends

1.19 A Friendly Adventure

Directions: Think about a time a friend and you shared an adventure. Answer the questions and write a narrative about your adventure. Be sure to include an opening, body, and closing in your writing. Support your ideas with details and examples.

1. Where did this adventure take place? _____

2. When did this adventure take place? _____

3. Who was with you? _____

4. Describe the scene of this adventure. _____

_____

_____

5. What happened? _____

_____

_____

6. How did the adventure end? _____

_____

_____

_____

1.20 A Friend in Need

Directions: Good friends are always willing to help each other. Think of a time you helped a friend. Answer the questions and write a narrative about this experience. Be sure to include an opening, body, and closing in your writing. Support your ideas with details and examples.

Among Friends

1. Who is your friend? _____

2. How long have you been friends? _____

3. When did you help your friend? _____

4. Why did he or she need help? _____

_____

_____

5. How did you help? _____

_____

_____

_____

6. What happened after you helped? _____

_____

_____

_____

_____

1.21 Friendly Letter

Directions: Think of a great novel or story you read. Now think of a friend who you believe would enjoy this book. Answer the questions; then write a letter to your friend to convince him or her to read this book. In your letter, try to show your friend why he or she would like this book, but do not reveal the book's ending.

1. What book would you like your friend to read? Who is the author?

   _____

2. Describe the main characters in the book. _____

   _____

   _____

3. Describe the book's plot (but do not reveal the ending). _____

   _____

   _____

4. Why did you like this book? _____

   _____

   _____

5. Why do you think your friend would like this book? _____

   _____

   _____

   _____

1.22 A Character Friend

Directions: Think of some favorite characters in some of your favorite stories or novels. Which of these characters would you most like to have as a friend? Answer the questions; then write an article explaining why this character would make a good friend. Be sure to include an opening, body, and closing in your writing. Support your ideas with details and examples.

1. What is the name of the character you would like to have as a friend?

    _____

2. What is the title of the story where you first "met" this character?

    _____

3. Describe the story. _____

    _____

    _____

4. Describe the character. _____

    _____

    _____

5. Explain what traits this character has that would make him or her a good friend.

1.23 A Biographical Sketch of a Friend

Directions: A *biography* is a true story of a person's life. A *biographical sketch* is a short biography. Answer the questions on this worksheet; then write a biographical sketch of a friend. Be sure to include an opening, body, and closing in your biography. Support your ideas with details and examples.

1. What is the name of your friend? _____

2. How old is your friend? _____

3. What is your friend's birthday? _____

4. Where was your friend born? _____

5. Describe your friend's family. _____

_____

6. Does your friend have any pets? If yes, describe them. _____

_____

7. Describe your friend. (Include what he or she likes and dislikes.)

_____

_____

8. What are your friend's plans for the future?

_____

_____

1.24 Secrets

1. What is your friend's name? _____

2. Describe him or her. _____

_____

3. Name and describe any other main characters in the story. _____

_____

4. What terrible secret does your friend share with you? _____

_____

5. What must you do? _____

_____

6. What happens next? _____

_____

_____

7. How does the story end? _____

_____

_____

1.25 When Friends Disagree

Directions: Imagine two friends who have a fight. What might happen? How might they feel? Answer the questions and write a story about two friends who have a fight. Be sure to include interesting characters, an exciting plot, and a climax to your story.

1. What are the names of the main characters in your story? _____

_____

2. Describe each of the main characters. _____

_____

3. Describe the setting of the story. _____

_____

4. When did the argument happen? _____

_____

5. What caused the fight? _____

_____

6. Describe the fight. _____

_____

7. What happened after the fight? _____

_____

1.26 My School

1. What is the name of your school? _____

2. What grades attend your school? _____

3. About how many students attend your school? _____

4. In what town and state is your school? _____

5. Describe your school (classrooms, gym, cafeteria, auditorium, playground, and so on). _____

_____

_____

6. What subjects do you learn in school? _____

_____

_____

7. Describe a typical school day. _____

_____

_____

_____

School Days

1.27 How to Improve My School

Directions: *Persuasive writing* is an article a person writes about a problem and how it might be solved. Think about the good things in your school. Now think about things that can be improved. Answer the questions and write a persuasive article about how your school can be improved. Be sure to include an opening, body, and closing in your writing. Support your ideas with details and examples.

1. Name something in your school that you feel should be improved.

   _____

2. Why should this be improved? Explain. _____

   _____

   _____

3. What could students do to help improve this? _____

   _____

   _____

4. What could teachers do to help improve this? _____

   _____

   _____

5. What could parents do to help improve this? _____

   _____

   _____

School Days

1.28 School Uniforms

Directions: Many schools have a dress code. Some schools even require that students wear uniforms. Think about your feelings about wearing a uniform to school. Answer the questions and write an article about your feelings. Be sure to include an opening, body, and closing in your writing. Support your ideas with details and examples.

1. Does your school require students to wear uniforms? If yes, describe the uniforms. _____

_____

_____

2. What are some advantages of wearing school uniforms? _____

_____

_____

_____

3. Why might students dislike wearing uniforms to school? _____

_____

_____

_____

4. What is your opinion about school uniforms? Explain. _____

_____

_____

_____

School Days

1.29 Guidelines for Picking a Student of the Month

1. What is the name of your award? _____

2. What is the award for? _____

_____

_____

_____

3. What will a student have to do to earn this award? _____

_____

_____

_____

4. What will the award be? _____

_____

_____

_____

School Days

1.30 School Food

Directions: School food is, well, school food. Most students eat it, but few like it. Imagine that you can choose the food your school will serve for lunch. Answer the questions and write an article about your choices for school lunches. (Try to choose healthy foods.) Be sure to include an opening, body, and closing in your writing. Support your ideas with details and examples.

1. What kinds of food does your school serve for lunch? _____

_____

_____

2. What foods would you like your school to serve for the main part of lunch?

_____

_____

3. What foods would you like for dessert? _____

_____

4. What types of beverages would you like served with lunch? _____

_____

_____

5. If your school has snack machines that students can use, what types of snacks should be offered?

_____

_____

_____

School Days

39

1.31 Should Students Have Homework?

Directions: Few students like homework. But most receive homework at least a few times each week. Think about how much homework you receive. Answer the questions and write an article explaining your feelings about homework. Remember to include an opening, body, and closing in your writing. Support your ideas with details and examples.

1. Why is homework important? _____

_____

_____

2. When might homework not be important? _____

_____

3. How much homework do you feel should be given each night? Explain.

_____

_____

4. Do you feel homework should be given on the weekends? Holidays? Explain. _____

_____

_____

5. Would it help or hurt students if they never got any homework? Explain.

_____

_____

1.32 Favorite Subjects

Directions: Think of all the subjects you are studying in school this year. Which are your favorites? Answer the questions and write an article about your favorite subjects. Be sure to include an opening, body, and closing in your writing. Support your ideas with details and examples.

1. List all the subjects you are studying this year. _____

_____

_____

2. Which are your favorites? _____

_____

_____

_____

3. Why are these your favorites? _____

_____

_____

_____

4. Do you ever use what you learn in these subjects outside of school?

   Explain. _____

_____

_____

_____

School Days

1.33 Should Schools Have Honor Rolls?

Directions: The purpose of an honor roll is to recognize students who achieve good grades. But some schools do not have honor rolls. People in these schools believe honor rolls are not needed. Does your school have an honor roll? If yes, should it be continued? If no, should one be started? Answer the questions; then write an article sharing your feelings about an honor roll in your school. Remember to include an opening, body, and closing in your writing. Support your ideas with details and examples.

1. List reasons why students may feel a school should have an honor roll.

_____

_____

_____

_____

2. List reasons why students may feel a school should not have an honor roll.

_____

_____

_____

_____

3. Should your school have an honor roll? Explain. _____

_____

_____

_____

1.34 A Description of My Classroom

1. Start at one corner and look around your classroom. List some of the objects you see. _____

_____

_____

_____

2. Write details of these objects (for example, size, shape, and color).

_____

_____

_____

3. Describe the furniture and how it is arranged. _____

_____

_____

_____

4. Describe any tables and study stations.

_____

_____

_____

1.35 A Review of an Exciting Program

1. What was the name of the program? _____

2. When and where was the program presented? _____

3. Who attended the program? _____

4. Who presented or starred in the program? _____

   _____

5. What was the program about? _____

   _____

6. Describe at least one thing you liked about the program. _____

   _____

7. Describe at least one thing you did not like about the program. _____

   _____

8. What was your opinion of the program? Explain. _____

   _____

   _____

1.36 The Best Things About My School

1. What do you feel is best about your school? _____

_____

2. Provide reasons and examples why you feel this way.

Reason 1: _____

_____

Example: _____

_____

Reason 2: _____

_____

Example: _____

_____

Reason 3: _____

_____

Example: _____

_____

School Days

1.37 My Classroom Rules

1. Describe your classroom (include grade, number of students, size, and so on). _____

   _____

   _____

2. Write at least three rules you would make to help your classroom run smoothly. _____

   _____

   _____

   _____

3. How would these rules help your classroom run smoothly? _____

   _____

   _____

   _____

4. Do you think most students would agree that your rules are helpful? Explain. _____

   _____

   _____

School Days

© Gary Robert Muschla

1.38 A New Student

Directions: Imagine that your teacher has chosen you to show a new student around your school. Answer the questions and write a story about this. Include interesting characters, a plot, and a climax in your story.

1. Who is the new student in your story? _____

2. Describe him or her. _____

   _____

   _____

3. How might a new student feel in a new school? _____

   _____

4. What places in your school would you show the new student?

   _____

5. Why would you take the new student to these places? _____

   _____

6. What (if anything) would you warn the new student about?

   _____

7. Will the new student like your school? Explain. _____

   _____

   _____

School Days

1.39 My Perfect School

1. Where would your school be located? _____

2. How long would your school day be? _____

3. How long would your school year be? _____

4. What grades would your school have? _____

5. About how many students would be in each class? _____

6. What subjects would students in your school learn? _____

_____

7. What special features would your school have? (For example, a big gymnasium, a swimming pool, a playground?) _____

_____

8. What would be the most important rule in your school? _____

_____

9. Would students receive a good education at your school? Explain.

_____

School Days

© Gary Robert Muschla

140 Home Sweet Home

Directions: Think about where you live and what makes your home different from anyone else's. Answer the questions and write a description of your home. Remember to include an opening, body, and closing in your writing. Support your ideas with details and examples.

1. Where do you live? _____

2. Describe your neighborhood or the area around your home. _____

_____

3. Describe the climate where you live. _____

_____

4. Describe your house or apartment. _____

_____

_____

5. What is special about your home? _____

_____

_____

6. Do you like living there? Why or why not? _____

_____

_____

_____

1.41 Around City and Town

1. List three places in your city or town (or in the area nearby) that visitors might be interested in seeing. _____

_____

_____

2. Describe each of these places. _____

_____

_____

_____

_____

_____

3. Why might newcomers enjoy visiting these places? _____

_____

4. What do you think visitors would like best about your city or town? _____

_____

_____

Near and Far

© Gary Robert Muschla

1.42 Traditions

Directions: Most cities and towns have special traditions. They might have a Founder's Day, a Memorial Day parade, or a fireworks display on the Fourth of July. Think about some of the traditions in the city or town where you live. Answer the questions and write an article about one of these traditions. Be sure to include an opening, body, and closing in your writing. Support your ideas with details and examples.

1. What is a tradition of your city or town? _____

_____

2. How often is this tradition celebrated? _____

3. Where is this tradition celebrated? _____

4. When is it celebrated? _____

5. Who takes an active part in the celebration? _____

_____

6. Describe this tradition or celebration. _____

_____

_____

7. What is your favorite part of this tradition? Explain. _____

_____

_____

Near and Far

1.43 Improvements

1. What is the name of your city or town? _____

2. Where is it located? _____

3. About how big is it? _____

4. Describe your city or town. _____

   _____

   _____

5. Name one thing that can be improved. _____

   _____

6. Why should this be improved? _____

   _____

   _____

7. How might it be improved? _____

   _____

   _____

1.44   The Best Food Around

Directions: Think about the best restaurant you have ever eaten at in your city or town. Answer the questions and write an article explaining why this place is the best place to eat. Remember to include an opening, body, and closing in your writing. Support your ideas with details and examples.

1. What is the name of the best restaurant in your city or town?

_____

2. Describe this place.   _____

_____

_____

3. With whom do you usually go to this place?   _____

4. What kinds of food are served there?   _____

_____

_____

5. Describe the best meal you have ever had there.   _____

_____

_____

6. Explain why this place is a popular place to eat.

_____

_____

1.45 An Interesting State

1. What is the subject of this article? _____

2. Where is this place located? _____

3. When did you visit this place? _____

4. With whom did you go? _____

5. Describe this place. _____

_____

_____

6. Why is it interesting? _____

_____

_____

_____

7. Would you like to visit this place again? Explain. _____

_____

_____

Near and Far

1.46 My Place

1. Where would you like to live? _____

2. Describe this place. _____

_____

_____

_____

3. Why would you like to live there? _____

_____

_____

4. What might be some disadvantages of living in this place? _____

_____

_____

_____

5. Do you think you would ever get tired of living in this place? Explain.

_____

_____

_____

Near and Far

1.47 The Best Vacation Ever!

Directions: Vacations can be times of great fun. Think of a vacation that you had. It might have been with your parents, relatives, or friends. Answer the questions and write a narrative about this vacation. Be sure to include an opening, body, and closing in your writing. Support your ideas with details and examples.

1. Where did you go for this vacation? _____

2. When did you go? _____

3. With whom did you go? _____

4. How did you get to your destination? _____

5. How long did you stay? _____

6. Describe the place you stayed at. _____

_____

_____

7. Describe what you did on your vacation. _____

_____

_____

8. What was the best part of your vacation? Explain.

_____

_____

1.48 A Travel First

Directions: Think back to a time when you first traveled in a train, sailed on a ship, flew in a plane, or maybe rode a horse. Answer the questions and write a narrative about this travel first. Be sure to include an opening, body, and closing in your writing. Support your ideas with details and examples.

1. What is the subject of your narrative?_____

2. How old were you when you first traveled in this way? _____

3. Where did you go? _____

4. Who was with you? _____

5. Describe your feelings about this travel first. _____

_____

_____

6. Did anything unusual happen on the trip? Explain. _____

_____

_____

7. Have you ever traveled like this again? If yes, explain how the other times

    were different from the first. _____

_____

_____

_____

Near and Far

1.49 Travel Advice

Directions: Imagine that a friend plans to go on vacation to a place that you have already visited. This might be a big amusement park, a cottage at a lake, or a large city. He or she asks you about this place and what to expect. Answer the questions; then write a letter of travel advice to your friend. Support your ideas with details and examples.

1. Where is your friend going on vacation? _____

2. What attractions might your friend expect to find there? _____

_____

3. Where would you suggest that he or she stay? Why? _____

_____

4. What kind of weather should your friend expect? _____

_____

5. What kinds of clothing should your friend bring? _____

_____

6. What types of equipment should your friend bring (for example,

   swimsuits, fishing poles, skis, sunglasses)? _____

_____

7. What would you warn your friend about? _____

_____

_____

Near and Far

© Gary Robert Muschla

1.50 Travel Calamity

1. Name and describe the main characters in your story. _____

_____

_____

2. Where are the characters going? _____

3. Why are they going there? _____

_____

4. How are they traveling there? _____

5. Describe at least one thing that goes wrong. _____

_____

6. How do they solve their problem? _____

_____

7. Do they reach their destination on time? Explain. _____

_____

Near and Far

1.51 Vacation Mystery

1. Where and when does this story take place? _____

2. Name and describe the main characters in your story (be sure to include yourself). _____

   _____

   _____

   _____

3. What is the mystery? _____

   _____

   _____

4. Name some clues that will help you solve the mystery. _____

   _____

   _____

5. How do you solve the mystery? _____

   _____

   _____

Near and Far

© Gary Robert Muschla

1.52 The Lost Puppy

Directions: Imagine that you or a friend has a puppy that gets lost. Answer the questions and write a story about how the puppy is found safe. Be sure to create interesting characters, an exciting plot, and a climax for your story.

1. Where and when does this story take place? _____

2. Name and describe the main characters. _____

_____

_____

3. Name and describe the puppy. _____

_____

_____

4. How does the puppy become lost? _____

_____

_____

5. How do the characters try to find the puppy? _____

_____

_____

6. How do they finally find the puppy? _____

_____

Near and Far

1.53 Stranger in Town

Directions: Imagine that a mysterious stranger comes to your town or neighborhood. This person has a secret. Answer the questions and write a story about this stranger. Be sure to create interesting characters, an exciting plot, and a climax for your story.

1. Where and when does the story take place? _____

2. Name and describe the main characters. _____

_____

_____

_____

3. What is unusual or mysterious about the stranger? _____

_____

_____

4. What secret does the stranger have? _____

_____

5. How do the other characters find out about the secret? _____

_____

6. How does the story end? _____

_____

_____

1.54 My Music

Directions: Think of your favorite kind of music. Answer the questions. Then write an article about the music you enjoy the most. Remember to include an opening, body, and closing in your writing. Support your ideas with details and examples.

1. What kind of music do you most like to listen to? _____

_____

2. Describe this type of music. _____

_____

3. What makes this type of music different from other kinds of music?

_____

4. Name some singers or groups who perform this type of music.

_____

5. Which is your favorite? Why? _____

_____

_____

6. Why do you like this type of music? Explain. _____

_____

_____

_____

Leisure Time

1.55 My Favorite Singer

1. Who is your favorite singer or musical group? _____

2. What type of music does this singer or group perform? _____

3. What do you feel is the best song of this singer or group? Why do you feel

    this is the best? _____

    _____

    _____

4. How is this singer or group different from others? _____

    _____

    _____

    _____

5. Why is this singer or group your favorite? Explain. _____

    _____

    _____

    _____

    _____

1.56 What the Song Says to Me

Directions: Most songwriters try to share ideas through their songs. The message they wish to share with their listeners is in the *lyrics* (or words) of the song. Choose a favorite song and think about the message of the songwriter. Answer the questions and write an article about what the song means to you. Be sure to include an opening, body, and closing in your writing. Support your ideas with details and examples.

1. What is the title of the song? _____

2. Who wrote and recorded the song? _____

3. What is the song about? _____

   _____

   _____

   _____

4. Which lyrics do you like the best? Why? _____

   _____

   _____

   _____

5. What is the message the songwriter is trying to share? Explain.

   _____

   _____

   _____

Leisure Time

1.57 A Book Review

1. What is the title of your book? _____

2. Who is the author? _____

3. Who is the publisher? _____

4. When was the book published? _____

5. Is this book fiction or nonfiction? _____

6. Explain what the book is about. (For fiction, tell about the setting, characters, and plot, but do not tell the ending.) _____

_____

_____

_____

_____

7. Did you like this book? Explain. _____

_____

_____

_____

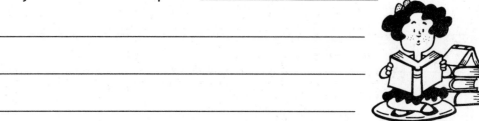

Leisure Time

© Gary Robert Muschla

1.58 Video Game Review

1. What is the name of the video game? _____

2. What age levels is it recommended for? _____

3. What must a player do to win? _____

   _____

4. Describe the action of the game. _____

   _____

   _____

   _____

5. What strategies can you suggest that will help a player to win?

   _____

   _____

6. Do you like this game? Why or why not? _____

   _____

   _____

Leisure Time

1.59 A Favorite Thing to Do

Directions: Think of something you enjoy doing—for example, sports, reading, or a hobby. Answer the questions and write an article about your favorite thing to do. Be sure to include an opening, body, and closing in your writing. Support your ideas with details and examples.

1. What is your favorite thing to do? _____

2. When and where do you enjoy this? _____

_____

_____

3. Describe your favorite thing to do. _____

_____

_____

_____

_____

_____

_____

4. Why is this your favorite thing to do? Explain. _____

_____

_____

_____

_____

1.60 A Most Special Day

Directions: Imagine you could spend a day doing anything you wished. What would you do? Answer the questions and write an article about this special day. Remember to include an opening, body, and closing in your writing. Support your ideas with details and examples.

1. Where would you go on this special day? _____

2. Why would you go there? _____

    _____

    _____

3. With whom would you spend this day? _____

    _____

4. Why would you choose this person or these people? _____

    _____

    _____

    _____

5. Describe all you would do on this special day. _____

    _____

    _____

    _____

    _____

Leisure Time

1.61 The Scariest Movie Ever!

1. What is the name of the movie? _____

2. What is the setting of the movie? _____

3. Who are the main characters? _____

_____

4. What is the movie about? _____

_____

_____

5. Describe the scariest scene. _____

_____

_____

6. Why do you think this scene is so scary? Explain. _____

_____

_____

7. Would you recommend this movie to your friends? Explain. _____

_____

1.62 TV in My Life

1. About how much TV do you watch each day? _____

2. Do you think the amount of TV you watch is too much, just about right, or too little? Explain. _____

   _____

3. What types of TV shows do you enjoy the most? Why? _____

   _____

   _____

4. What types of TV shows do you enjoy the least? Why? _____

   _____

   _____

5. What is good about TV? Explain. _____

   _____

   _____

6. What is not good about TV? Explain. _____

   _____

   _____

Leisure Time

1.63 Character Changes

1. What is the title of the story? _____

2. What is the name of the character? _____

3. Describe the story. _____

_____

4. Describe the character at the beginning of the story. _____

_____

_____

5. Describe the character at the end of the story. _____

_____

_____

6. Describe the changes in the character. _____

_____

7. What caused these changes? Explain. _____

_____

1.64 A Fantasy Lunch

1. With whom would you have lunch? _____

2. Why would you choose this person? _____

   _____

3. Where would you have lunch? _____

4. What would you have for lunch? _____

   _____

   _____

5. If you could ask this person three questions, what would they be?

   _____

   _____

   _____

6. What do you think the answers would be? _____

   _____

   _____

   _____

Leisure Time

1.65 A Great Product

1. What is the product? _____

2. Where can people buy this product? _____

3. Describe what the product does. _____

_____

_____

_____

_____

4. Why are you so pleased with this product? _____

_____

_____

_____

5. What, if anything, could make this product even better? Explain.

_____

_____

_____

Leisure Time

© Gary Robert Muschla

74

1.66 Changing Places

1. What is the title of the story you are in? _____

2. Which character did you replace? _____

3. Name and describe the main characters in the story. _____

_____

_____

_____

4. Summarize the original story. _____

_____

_____

_____

_____

5. Describe the new ending. _____

_____

_____

_____

Leisure Time

1.67 The Un-Fun Funhouse

Directions: Imagine going in a funhouse that had no way out. Answer the questions and write a story about how you escaped this frightening funhouse. Create interesting characters, an exciting plot, and a climax for your story.

1. Where is the funhouse located? _____

2. Name and describe the main characters in your story. _____

_____

_____

3. Describe the funhouse. _____

_____

_____

_____

4. Why were you unable to find your way out? _____

_____

_____

_____

5. How did you finally escape the funhouse? _____

_____

_____

_____

1.68 The Game

Directions: Think of a game you like to play. It might be a board game, a playground game, or a card game. Answer the questions and write an article about this game. Be sure to include an opening, body, and closing in your writing. Support your ideas with details and examples.

1. What is the name of this game? _____

2. When did you learn to play this game? _____

3. Who taught you how to play? _____

4. How many people can play the game at the same time? _____

5. Does the game require teams? Explain. _____

_____

6. Describe the game (include its basic rules and how you win).

_____

_____

7. What strategies might someone use to win? _____

_____

8. Why do you enjoy this game? Explain. _____

_____

_____

1.69 My Favorite Sport

1. What is your favorite sport? _____

2. Explain which you enjoy doing more: playing or watching this sport.

   _____

3. If teams are necessary, how many players are on a team? _____

4. Explain what, if any, special positions the team has. _____

   _____

5. Where is this sport played? _____

6. What equipment do you need for this sport? _____

   _____

7. Describe how a game is played in this sport. _____

   _____

   _____

8. Why do you like this sport? _____

   _____

   _____

1.70 Superstars

1. Who is the superstar athlete? _____

2. In which sport is he or she a superstar? _____

3. Does this athlete play on a team? If yes, which one? _____

4. What position does he or she play? _____

5. How is this athlete more skilled than others who play this sport?

_____

6. What, if any, championships has this athlete won? _____

_____

7. What, if any, records has he or she broken? _____

_____

8. What makes this athlete a superstar? _____

_____

_____

1.71 A Perfect Day

Directions: Imagine that you could have a perfect day. You could go wherever you wanted and do whatever you wanted. Answer the questions and write about this perfect day. Remember to include an opening, body, and closing in your writing. Support your ideas with details and examples.

Morning

1. Where would you go? _____

2. Who would be with you? _____

3. What would you do? _____

Afternoon

1. Where would you go? _____

2. Who would be with you? _____

3. What would you do? _____

Evening

1. Where would you go? _____

2. Who would be with you? _____

3. What would you do? _____

What would be the most special part of the day? Why? _____

_____

1.72 Playground Safety

Directions: Imagine that you could write safety rules for your school's or neighborhood's playground. Answer the questions and write an article explaining your playground rules. Be sure to include an opening, body, and closing in your writing. Support your ideas with details and examples.

1. Do playgrounds need safety rules? Explain. _____

_____

2. What is the first rule you would want for a playground? Why is this rule

   important? _____

_____

_____

3. What is a second rule? Why is this rule important? _____

_____

_____

4. What is a third rule? Why is this rule important? _____

_____

_____

5. What might happen if people do not follow rules when using the

   equipment on a playground? Explain. _____

_____

_____

1.73 The Best

Directions: Think of a time you were at your best. Maybe you were playing a game, such as soccer. Maybe you were playing in the school band at a concert. Maybe you were fishing with your grandfather and caught the biggest fish. Whatever you were doing, you were at your very best. Answer the questions and write a narrative about this day. Remember to include an opening, body, and closing in your writing. Support your ideas with details and examples.

1. What were you doing when you were at your best? _____

_____

_____

2. When and where were you at your best? _____

3. Who was with you? _____

4. Describe what made this day your best at what you were doing.

_____

_____

5. Describe how you felt being your best. _____

_____

_____

6. Did others realize you were at your best? Explain. _____

_____

1.74 Talent or Desire

Directions: Think about playing sports, playing a musical instrument, dancing, or being a cheerleader. What is more important to being successful, talent or desire? Answer the questions and write an article about which is more important. Be sure to include an opening, body, and closing in your writing. Support your ideas with details and examples.

1. What must a person do to become successful at sports, music, or other activities? _____

_____

_____

2. How important is talent to being successful? Explain. _____

_____

_____

3. How important is desire to being successful? Explain. _____

_____

_____

_____

4. What, if any, other things might be important? Explain. _____

_____

_____

_____

_____

1.75 A Thrilling Time

Directions: Think of a time you were at a thrilling event. For example, this might have been a championship football game, a cheerleading competition, or a monster truck show. Answer the questions and write about this time. Remember to include an opening, body, and closing in your writing. Support your ideas with details and examples.

1. What was this time? _____

2. Where and when did it take place? _____

3. Who was with you? _____

4. Describe the time. _____

_____

_____

_____

5. What was the most thrilling part of the time? Why? _____

_____

_____

_____

6. What was the least thrilling part of the time? Why? _____

_____

_____

_____

1.76 A New Game

Directions: Have you ever invented a game or created new rules for an old game? Answer the questions; then write an article about a new game, or a new version of an old game, you invented. Remember to include an opening, body, and closing in your writing. Support your ideas with details and examples.

1. What is the name of your new game? _____

2. When did you invent this game? _____

3. Who, if anyone, helped you invent the game? _____

4. Describe the game and its rules. _____

   _____

   _____

   _____

   _____

5. How does a player win? _____

   _____

   _____

6. Have you played this game with others? If yes, did they like the game?
   Explain. _____

   _____

   _____

1.77 Being a Good Sport

Directions: Think about what it means to be a good sport. Answer the questions and write an article about being a good sport. Be sure to include an opening, body, and closing in your writing. Support your ideas with details and examples.

1. What does being a "good sport" mean? _____

_____

_____

_____

2. Give at least three examples of being a good sport. _____

_____

_____

_____

3. Is being a good sport important? Explain. _____

_____

_____

_____

4. Which is more important—winning or being a good sport? Explain.

_____

_____

_____

1.78 Report on a Sports Product

> **Directions:** Think of sports equipment, such as a baseball glove, ice skates, or sneakers. Answer the questions; then write an article about a sports product, telling about its strengths and weaknesses. Be sure to include an opening, body, and closing in your writing. Support your ideas with details and examples.

1. What product is the subject of your article? _____

2. How often do you use this product? _____

3. Describe this product. _____

_____

_____

4. What do you like about this product? _____

_____

_____

5. What do you dislike about it? _____

_____

_____

6. Would you recommend this product to others? Explain. _____

_____

_____

_____

1.79 Special Doings

Directions: Think of a special activity that you enjoy with family or friends. Maybe you ride roller coasters with your cousin. Maybe you swim with friends in your pool. Or maybe you go camping with your parents. Answer the questions and write a narrative about your special doings. Remember to include an opening, body, and closing in your writing. Support your ideas with details and examples.

1. What is your special activity? _____

2. Who does this activity with you? _____

3. Where and when do you enjoy this special activity? _____

_____

4. Describe this activity. _____

_____

_____

_____

_____

5. What makes this activity special? Explain. _____

_____

_____

_____

_____

1.80 Great Competition

> **Directions:** Think of a time you were in a great competition. Maybe you were in a dance competition. Maybe you were playing a tough computer game. Maybe you were in a race on the playground. Answer the questions and write a narrative about this great competition. Be sure to include an opening, body, and closing in your writing. Support your ideas with details and examples.

1. What was the competition? _____

2. Whom were you competing against? _____

3. When and where was this competition? _____

_____

4. Describe the competition. _____

_____

_____

5. What strategies did you use to try to win? _____

_____

_____

6. How did you win? Or why did you lose? Explain. _____

_____

_____

_____

1.81 Hey, Coach

Directions: Imagine that you are a coach. You might be a soccer coach, a cheerleading coach, or a dance instructor. What advice could you give to younger students? Answer the questions and write an article about the advice you would give. Be sure to include an opening, body, and closing in your writing. Support your ideas with details and examples.

1. What sport or activity are you coaching? _____

2. How much experience do you have with this activity? _____

   _____

   _____

3. What do you like about this activity? _____

   _____

   _____

4. What skills should students have if they want to do well in this activity?

   _____

   _____

5. What advice would you give to younger students who are just starting this activity? _____

   _____

   _____

   _____

1.82 The Big Game

1. What is the game in this story? _____

2. Name and describe the main characters. _____

_____

_____

3. Where and when does this story take place? _____

_____

4. How does the story begin? _____

_____

5. List three important things that happen in the story. _____

_____

_____

_____

6. Describe how the story ends. _____

_____

_____

1.83 UFOs (Unidentified Flying Objects)

1. Have you ever seen a UFO? If yes, where and when? _____

_____

2. Describe the UFO you saw. _____

_____

3. If you have not seen a UFO, do you believe they exist? Explain.

_____

4. Do you believe that life exists on other planets? If yes, explain why.

_____

_____

5. Do you believe beings from other planets have visited Earth? Explain.

_____

_____

6. If you do not believe that UFOs exist or that intelligent beings may live on other planets, explain why. _____

_____

_____

1.84 Unexplained!

Directions: Everybody has seen or heard about strange events that cannot be explained. Answer the questions; then write about an unexplained event you have seen or heard about. Remember to include an opening, body, and closing in your writing. Support your ideas with details and examples.

1. What was the event? _____

2. Where and when did it happen? _____

_____

_____

3. Who was with you? _____

4. Describe the event. _____

_____

_____

_____

5. How did you, or others, try to explain what happened? _____

_____

_____

6. Why did the event remain unexplained? _____

_____

_____

1.85 Nightmare!

1. Who is in your nightmare? _____

_____

_____

2. Where are you in your nightmare? _____

3. Describe the setting of your nightmare. _____

_____

4. Describe what happens in your nightmare. _____

_____

_____

_____

_____

5. Do you wake up during your nightmare? If yes, how do you feel?

_____

6. Are you afraid to go back to sleep after waking up? Why? _____

_____

1.86 Do You Believe in Magic?

> **Directions:** Imagine being given magic powers, but your powers will allow you to cast only one magic spell. Answer the questions and write a story about your magic power. Create interesting characters, an exciting plot, and a climax for your story.

1. Name and describe the characters in your story. _____

   _____

2. Where and when does the story take place? _____

   _____

3. How did you receive your magic powers? _____

   _____

   _____

4. What one act of magic do you perform? _____

   _____

   _____

5. Why do you perform this act? _____

   _____

6. What happens after you perform your magic? _____

   _____

   _____

Weird, Strange, and Unbelievable

1.87 It's a Dog's Life

> **Directions:** Imagine if your dog, or another animal who knows you, could read and write. Now imagine if your dog kept a diary. Answer the questions and write a diary entry as if the entry had been written by your dog. Be sure to include great details in your writing.

1. Describe what your dog sees throughout the day. _____

_____

2. Describe what your dog hears throughout the day. _____

_____

3. Describe what your dog does most of the day. _____

_____

4. Describe what the best part of your dog's day is. _____

_____

_____

5. Describe what the worst part of your dog's day is. _____

_____

_____

6. Describe what your dog would say about you in the diary. _____

_____

_____

1.88 Reporter in the Past

Directions: Imagine that you are a reporter living in the past. You are writing about an important event that happened. Answer the questions and write an article about this event. Be sure to include an opening, body, and closing in your writing. Support your ideas with details and examples.

1. What event are you writing about? _____

2. When did this event take place? _____

3. Where did it take place? _____

4. Who was involved in the event? _____

_____

5. Describe the event. _____

_____

_____

6. Why did the event happen? _____

_____

_____

7. What happened after the event? _____

_____

_____

Weird, Strange, and Unbelievable

1.89 Coming Disaster

1. Where and when does your story take place? _____

_____

2. Name and describe the main characters in your story. _____

_____

_____

3. Describe the disaster that is about to happen. _____

_____

_____

4. What will you do to stop the disaster? _____

_____

_____

_____

5. Are you successful? Why or why not? _____

_____

_____

_____

Weird, Strange, and Unbelievable

1.90 Extraterrestrials in My School

Directions: Imagine that extraterrestrials, beings from another planet, have come to Earth. They are friendly and wish to learn about us. Some extraterrestrial students are visiting your school. You have been asked to show them around. Answer the questions and write a story about the extraterrestrials in your school. Create interesting characters, an exciting plot, and a climax for your story.

1. Name and describe the extraterrestrials who come to your school.

   _____

2. Where did the extraterrestrials come from? _____

   _____

3. Name and describe the human characters in your story. _____

   _____

4. Why were you chosen to show the extraterrestrials around? _____

   _____

5. What did you show them? _____

   _____

   _____

6. What did they find most interesting about your school? _____

   _____

   _____

1.91 Video Game Hero

Directions: Think of your favorite video game. Imagine you are the star character of the game. Answer the questions and write a story about being a hero in a video game. Create interesting characters, an exciting plot, and a climax for your story.

1. What is the name of the video game? _____

2. Describe the setting of the game. _____

_____

3. Name and describe the main characters in the game. _____

_____

4. Describe the purpose of the game. _____

_____

5. Describe your attempts to win the game. _____

_____

6. How do your opponents try to stop you? _____

_____

_____

7. Do you win the game? Explain. _____

_____

_____

1.92 Oh, No! Enchanted!

Directions: Imagine that an evil witch casts a spell on you. This spell forces you to say whatever you are thinking. Answer the questions and write a story about this terrible spell. Create interesting characters, an exciting plot, and a climax for your story.

1. Name and describe the main characters in your story. _____

_____

2. Where and when does the story take place? _____

_____

3. How did you become enchanted? _____

_____

4. When did you realize you were enchanted? _____

_____

5. Describe how the spell got you in trouble. _____

_____

_____

_____

6. How did you manage to break the spell? _____

_____

_____

Weird, Strange, and Unbelievable

1.93 Me—Home Alone

1. When were you home alone? _____

2. Why were you home alone? _____

3. What were you doing when you first heard the strange, frightening sounds? _____

_____

4. Where did the sounds come from? _____

5. Describe the sounds. _____

_____

6. Describe your feelings when you heard the sounds. _____

_____

7. What did you do after hearing the sounds? _____

_____

8. Did you find out what was making the sounds? Explain. _____

_____

_____

Weird, Strange, and Unbelievable

1.94 A Big Switch

Directions: Imagine that you could switch places with a plant or an animal for a day. You would become that plant or animal for twenty-four hours. Answer the questions and write a story about your experience. Create interesting characters, an exciting plot, and a climax for your story.

1. What plant or animal would you switch places with? Why? _____

_____

_____

2. Where would you be after switching places? _____

_____

3. Describe your "new" self. _____

_____

_____

4. Describe what you would see, hear, feel, smell, and taste. _____

_____

_____

_____

5. What would be the strangest thing about switching places?

_____

1.95 Super Running Shoes

Directions: Imagine that you were given a pair of running shoes that made you the fastest runner in the world. Answer the questions and write a story about these super running shoes. Create interesting characters, an exciting plot, and a climax for your story.

1. Name and describe the characters in your story. _____

_____

2. Where and when does this story take place? _____

_____

3. Who gave you the running shoes? _____

4. Why did this person give them to you? _____

_____

5. How did you discover their super speed? _____

_____

6. What did you do after you learned about their speed? _____

_____

_____

7. What eventually happened to the super running shoes? _____

_____

_____

1.96 Back to the Past

1. Name and describe the main characters of your story. _____

    _____

2. How do you return to the past? _____

    _____

3. Describe the past you return to. _____

    _____

    _____

4. Knowing the things you know now, would you change anything in the

    past? If yes, what? If no, why not? _____

    _____

    _____

    _____

5. Would any changes you made in the past change the present? Explain.

    _____

    _____

    _____

Weird, Strange, and Unbelievable

1.97 Talking Teddy

Directions: Imagine a teddy bear, or another stuffed animal, suddenly beginning to talk. Answer the questions and write a story about this talking stuffed animal. Create interesting characters, an exciting plot, and a climax for your story.

1. Describe the stuffed animal. _____

   _____

2. When does it begin to talk? _____

3. Why does it begin to talk? _____

   _____

4. What does it say? _____

   _____

5. What do you do when it begins to talk? _____

   _____

6. Does anyone else know the stuffed animal can talk? _____

7. Do you tell anyone about the talking stuffed animal? Explain. _____

   _____

8. Does the stuffed animal eventually stop talking? Explain. _____

   _____

1.98 Fantasy Pet

Directions: Imagine being able to have a fantasy pet—for example, a dragon, a unicorn, or a giant eagle you can fly on. Answer the questions and write a story about your fantasy pet. Create interesting characters, an exciting plot, and a climax for your story.

1. Name and describe your fantasy pet. _____

_____

_____

2. Name and describe the main characters in your story. _____

_____

_____

3. Where and when does the story take place? _____

_____

4. How did you get your fantasy pet? _____

_____

_____

5. What do you and your fantasy pet do together? _____

_____

_____

_____

_____

1.99 Ancient Artifact

1. Name and describe the main characters in your story. _____

_____

2. Where and when does this story take place? _____

_____

3. Describe the artifact you find. _____

_____

4. What are its special powers? _____

_____

5. How do you learn of these powers? _____

_____

6. What happens after you learn of its powers? _____

_____

7. Do you keep the artifact? Or do you return it to the cave so that no one else can find it? Explain. _____

_____

Weird, Strange, and Unbelievable

© Gary Robert Muschla

1.100 Invisible Me

Directions: Imagine that you gain the power to make yourself invisible. But this power lasts only a day. Answer the questions and write a story about when you were invisible. Create interesting characters, an exciting plot, and a climax for your story.

1. Name and describe the main characters in your story. _____
_____

2. Where and when does this story take place? _____
_____

3. How do you gain the power to become invisible? _____
_____

4. How do you feel when you are invisible? _____
_____

5. Describe what you do when you are invisible. _____
_____
_____

6. Does anyone know about your power? Explain. _____
_____

7. What happens when your power begins to weaken? _____
_____

Weird, Strange, and Unbelievable

Writing the Draft

Writing the draft is the part of the writing process in which ideas are put into words. It is the real work of writing.

Expressing ideas is a big step beyond coming up with ideas. A first draft is only the first attempt of what may turn out to be many attempts at completing a piece. Few writers get a draft "right" the first time, or the second, or the third. Professional authors may work through a dozen or more drafts. Even then they may not be satisfied that they expressed their ideas in the best way possible. A draft should be considered as but one step forward in finishing a piece.

For many writers the draft is a time of discovery. Some drafts closely follow the ideas that the writer has already formulated. Others lead the writer to new ideas. Some are written quickly with high energy and emotion. Others are written in a series of starts and stops because the writer has trouble finding his way. Some surprise the writer with unexpected insights. Others are disappointing and force the writer to return to his original ideas to figure out what is wrong. Throughout all this, it is the writer's decisions that guide the development of the draft.

You should look at a draft as a testing ground where you can examine your ideas and decide if you are writing exactly what you wish to say. You should see each draft as an opportunity that leads you closer to the clear expression of ideas.

Writing a draft is hard work. Writing becomes easier when you understand the fundamentals of sentences, paragraphs, and good technique.

Sentences: The Foundation of the Draft

To write well, you must have a basic knowledge and understanding of sentences. This understanding must include the four types of sentences—*declarative, interrogative, imperative,* and *exclamatory*—as well as *simple, compound,* and *complex* sentence structures. Understanding sentence types and structures will help you to write clearly.

Exercise 2.1 Types of Sentences

Study the following sentences:

- Rashad walked to school. (declarative)
- Did Susan finish her homework? (interrogative)
- Close the window. (imperative)
- Watch out! (exclamatory)

A *declarative* sentence is a statement and requires a period. An *interrogative* sentence is a question and requires a question mark. An *imperative* sentence is a command or request and requires a period. An *exclamatory* sentence expresses great emotion and requires an exclamation point.

A sentence must contain a *subject* and a *predicate* to express a complete thought. In the declarative sentence, *Rashad* is the subject and *walked* is the predicate. In the interrogative sentence, *Susan* is the subject and *did finish* is the predicate. In the imperative sentence, *close* is the predicate and the subject is understood to be *you*, the person to whom the command is directed. *You* (understood) is also the subject of the exclamatory sentence, in which *watch* is the predicate. Write examples of your own and identify the subjects and predicates.

Exercise 2.2 Sentence Structures

Study the following examples of sentence structures.

- Maria plays the flute in the school band. (simple)
- Sam enjoys sports, but his sister loves music. (compound)
- Whenever it snows, Will goes snowboarding. (complex)

The examples are three common sentence structures. Understanding these structures will help you to use different forms of sentences in your writing.

The first example is a simple sentence. It has one subject, *Maria*, and one predicate, *plays*.

The second example is a compound sentence. In a compound sentence, two separate sentences are connected with the words *and, but, or,* or *nor.* Note the subject, *Sam*, and the predicate, *enjoys*, in the first sentence. Note the subject, *sister*, and the predicate, *loves*, in the second. Also note that *but* is the connecting word.

The third example is a complex sentence. A complex sentence has one independent clause, which can stand alone as a simple sentence, and one dependent clause, which cannot. In the example, *whenever it snows* is the dependent clause, and *Will goes snowboarding* is the independent clause. (Independent clauses are also called main clauses, and dependent clauses are also called subordinate clauses.)

By using all three forms of sentences you will be able to vary your writing and present your ideas in an interesting manner. Write some examples of your own and identify the sentence structure of each. For additional practice with sentences, do Worksheets 2.1 and 2.2 at the end of this section.

Exercise 2.3 Combining and Varying Sentences

Study these examples:

After school Ashley did her homework. She went shopping with her mother. She went to dance practice.

These are three simple sentences. Although they are written correctly, they are flat and boring. Imagine a whole article or story written like this. Short sentences like these can be combined to make writing smoother and more interesting. See the following example:

After school Ashley did her homework, went shopping with her mother, and went to dance practice.

Here is another example:

The night sky darkened. The stars appeared and began to twinkle.

These sentences can be combined and rewritten slightly, but with the result showing a big difference:

As the night sky darkened, the stars appeared and began to twinkle.

Combining and varying sentences makes writing more interesting for readers. For additional practice, do Worksheets 2.3 and 2.4 at the end of this section.

Building Paragraphs

A well-written paragraph is constructed of sentences related to one main idea. The paragraph contains a topic sentence that states the main idea of the paragraph. Other sentences support the main idea with details and examples.

Although the topic sentence is the first sentence in most paragraphs, it may appear in the middle or at the end. Many writers find that placing the topic sentence at the beginning of the paragraph makes it easier to organize the paragraph and provide details.

Paragraphs may vary in length, depending on their main idea and supporting details. A paragraph must be long enough to fully develop its main idea.

Many students use general main ideas or supporting ideas that lack details. Try to develop your paragraphs one sentence at a time, starting with the topic sentence, and then support it with details and examples.

Exercise 2.4 Constructing Paragraphs

Study this example of an undeveloped paragraph:

The movie was great. It was the best movie I ever saw.

Although it is clear the writer liked the movie, he or she offers no supporting details. The absence of supporting ideas weakens the main idea. What kinds of details could be included that would support and strengthen the main idea in this paragraph? Possible details include the following:

- The title of the movie
- The type of movie
- The actors and actresses and how they helped to make the movie great
- A brief description of the plot and how it helped to make the movie great
- Why the author liked the movie

Exercise 2.5 Reviewing Paragraphs

Choose two or three descriptive paragraphs from your reading book or science or social studies text. Read the paragraphs. For each one, identify the main idea. Find the topic sentence and the supporting details. Notice how details support and expand the main idea.

Concentrate on building solid paragraphs in your writing. Remember to organize each paragraph around a main idea. Express that idea in a topic sentence and provide supporting details. For additional practice with paragraphs, do Worksheets 2.5, 2.6, and 2.7 at the end of this section.

Showing and Not Telling

Good writers understand that they must show and not tell about ideas in their writing. Because showing requires action, authors who show, and do not only tell, write with clearer imagery.

Exercise 2.6 Show, Show, Show

Study this example to see the power of showing over telling:

- When the toy broke, the little boy was upset. (telling)
- When the toy broke, the little boy stamped his foot and started to cry. (showing)

In the first sentence, the writer tells that the *boy was upset.* In the second sentence, *stamped his foot and started to cry* shows that the boy was upset. Showing provides action that the reader can visualize in her imagination, making the idea clear.

Here is another example:

- The sunset was pretty. (telling)
- The sun drifted lower in the bright red sky. (showing)

The second sentence provides action—*The sun drifted lower*—and visual details—*in the bright red sky*—that sharpen the idea of the sun setting. The second sentence is an example of stronger writing than the first.

Write some examples of your own that show rather than tell.

For more practice, do Worksheet 2.8 at the end of this section.

Using Adjectives and Adverbs Wisely

Adjectives and adverbs are useful for adding details to writing. But many students use too many adjectives and adverbs. Some overuse these modifiers thinking that more details will make their writing better. The opposite is true. Too many adjectives and adverbs weaken writing. Adjectives and adverbs should be used only when necessary.

Following are some examples of unnecessary adjectives and adverbs:

- green grass (Unless the grass is dead or the season is winter, grass is green.)
- totally surprised (Can someone be partially surprised?)
- completely fooled (A person is either fooled or not fooled.)
- happy smile (Most smiles arise from happiness. The exception is a sad smile.)

While adjectives and adverbs have a purpose in sentences, they should be chosen with care. Instead of bland modifiers, you should seek ones that provide sharp details.

To gain an understanding and appreciation of the use of adjectives and adverbs, find examples in your reading. Notice how the proper use of adjectives or adverbs can strengthen writing. For practice using adjectives and adverbs wisely in your writing, do Worksheets 2.9, 2.10, and 2.11 at the end of this section.

Order and Sequence

In real life, things happen in order. All the things we do are part of a long sequence of cause and effect. In the same way, articles and stories must have order. Even stories that include flashbacks follow a plan of order.

Problems with order usually arise from one of two causes: 1) The writer is not paying attention to order because he wants to finish the writing as fast as possible or 2) He is so enthused with expressing his ideas that attention to order is lost. Good writing shows a sequential development of ideas in an ordered structure.

To gain an understanding of order and sequence, find order and sequence in the stories and articles you read. Notice how ideas develop logically, how ideas are related, and how ideas are presented in sequence.

Concentrate on the order of ideas in your writing. For most pieces ideas should build logically from start to end. For most writers a chronological sequence provides a practical order. If you have trouble maintaining a logical order in your writing, write a list of your ideas according to time. Checking your list as you write will help you to follow a consistent sequence. For practice on order and sequence, do Worksheet 2.12 at the end of this section.

Using Active Constructions

Active constructions, sometimes referred to as *active voice*, help to make writing direct and strong. Passive constructions, also known as *passive voice*, make writing indirect and weak. Active constructions are clear and add force to writing. Study the following example:

- Jimmy finished his homework. (active)
- The homework was finished by Jimmy. (passive)

Notice that the active construction is shorter and provides a clear idea. The passive construction is wordy. In the active construction, *Jimmy* is the subject and *finished* is the predicate. There is no confusion that Jimmy finished the homework. In the passive construction, *homework* is the subject and the predicate is the phrase *was finished. Jimmy* becomes the object of the preposition *by*. Most readers easily understand the first sentence. Some have to think about the meaning of the second. Active constructions are almost always a better choice than passive constructions because they help readers to visualize action and ideas.

Exercise 2.7 Active Versus Passive Constructions

Study the following example:

- Jamal hit a home run. (active)
- A home run was hit by Jamal. (passive)

In the first sentence the action is clear. Although the second sentence says the same thing, the action is not expressed as clearly. This is the major difference between active and passive constructions: active constructions are clear and direct; passive constructions are wordy and less clear.

Here is another example:

- Larissa smiled at the baby. (active)
- The baby was smiled at by Larissa. (passive)

The first sentence is the active construction. For practice with active and passive constructions, do Worksheet 2.13 at the end of this section.

Using Strong Verbs

Closely linked to active constructions are strong verbs. Like active constructions, strong verbs paint clear pictures in the imaginations of readers. English is a vast, rich language. We have words for just about everything, and we have exact verbs for all kinds of action.

Exercise 2.8 Strong Verbs

Study the following pairs of sentences:

- The wind was powerful.
- The wind gusted.

- The squirrel went up the tree.
- The squirrel scampered up the tree.

- The little girl called loudly for her brother.
- The little girl shouted for her brother.

The second sentence of each pair uses a strong verb to show the action. Strong verbs result in writing that is less wordy. For practice with strong verbs, do Worksheet 2.14 at the end of this section.

Verb Tenses

The tense of a verb shows when something happens, or happened, in a sentence. The three most commonly used tenses are *present*, *past*, and *future*.

Following are examples of each tense:

- Verbs in the present tense show action that is happening now. *Sandra walks to school each day.*
- Verbs in the past tense show action that has happened. *Sandra walked to school yesterday.*
- Verbs in the future tense show action that will happen. *Sandra will walk to school tomorrow.*

Most writers use the past tense, because the events they are writing about have already happened. This is especially true for stories and most articles. In some articles—for example, essays and editorials—an author may want to express a feeling that the subject of the article is currently happening. In such cases, the author uses present tense.

You must choose the correct tense for the stories and articles you write. A narrative, for example, based on a past event, requires the past tense. An article about the lunches currently served in the school cafeteria might be written in the present tense.

Once a tense is chosen, be careful not to shift tenses unnecessarily. Sometimes writers start in the past tense, then switch to the present, only to switch back to the past. This can be confusing to readers. Tense shifts can undermine expression and weaken ideas. For practice with verb tenses, do Worksheet 2.15 at the end of this section.

Subject-Verb Agreement

A subject and verb of a sentence must always agree. In the present tense, singular subjects require the singular form of verbs. Plural subjects require the plural form of verbs. In the past tense the forms of verbs are the same for singular and plural subjects. The only exception is the verb *be*. The singular past tense form of *be* is *was* and the plural past tense form is *were*.

Exercise 2.9 Agreement

Study these examples:

- Tim walks to school each day. (present tense)
- Tim and Sancho walk to school each day. (present tense)
- Tim walked to school yesterday. (past tense)
- Tim and Sancho walked to school yesterday. (past tense)

Find the subjects and verbs in the sentences. In the present tense, the singular subject *Tim* requires the singular form of the verb *walk*, which is *walks*. The plural subjects *Tim* and *Sancho* require the plural form, *walk*. When using the past tense, both singular and plural subjects use the same form, *walked*. For additional practice with subject-verb agreement, do Worksheet 2.16 at the end of this section.

Point of View

Point of view (POV) is the way an author tells a story. The two most common points of view are the *first person point of view* and the *third person point of view*. Most writers use one of these points of view in their writing.

In the first person POV, the author is a participant in or observer of the action. The author tells the story or writes about an event firsthand. The author refers to herself as "I." Many students find the first person POV easier to write with because they can use their own voice. It is also easier to write with emotion and feeling in the first person POV. The major disadvantage of this POV is that it limits writing, especially for stories. The author, as participant in and narrator of the story, can write only about what she experiences in the story. For example, while writing in the first person POV, the author cannot describe the thoughts or feelings of another character.

In the third person POV, the author writes from outside the piece. The author is not a part of the action. Characters are referred to as "he" or "she." The third person POV allows the author broader control of the piece. Most writing is done in the third person POV.

You must write with a consistent POV. Do not start a story in the first person, switch to the third, then switch back to the first, only to switch once again to the third. Unexpected switches between the first and third person POVs confuse readers. Stories and articles that suffer POV switches quickly lose focus. Ideas become unclear and writing loses direction.

To gain an understanding of POV, look for POV in your reading and think about why authors chose the POV they did. As you learn to recognize POV in your reading, you will use POV effectively in your writing. For practice with POV, do Worksheets 2.17 and 2.18 at the end of this section.

Comparison and Contrast

Comparing and *contrasting* are tools that allow writers to identify the similarities and differences between things. They help writers to highlight details. Comparing and contrasting help to make ideas clear.

Comparing shows similarities and contrasting shows differences. You should use comparison and contrast whenever you need to show how two ideas are alike and different.

There are two methods for comparing and contrasting. In method one, the author describes the first idea fully, then describes the second fully, showing how they are alike and different. In method two, the author describes one feature of the first idea and compares and contrasts it to the same feature of the second idea. The author then compares and contrasts the second feature, then the third, and so on.

Exercise 2.10 Comparing and Contrasting Pets

Think about the topics "cat" and "dog." To compare and contrast cats and dogs, ask yourself how cats and dogs are alike and different. Some similarities might include the following:

- Both animals are mammals.
- Both are popular as pets.
- As pets they can become "members of the family."

Differences might include the following:

- Dogs are more playful; cats like to "do their own thing."
- Cats purr when contented; dogs wag their tails.
- Cats meow; dogs bark.

These are just some possibilities and it is likely you will come up with more.

Use comparing and contrasting in your own writing. For additional practice with comparison and contrast, do Worksheet 2.19 at the end of this section.

Figurative Language

Figurative language can turn good writing into great writing. Figures of speech include *similes*, *metaphors*, and *personification*.

Similes make comparisons using the words *like* or *as*. Metaphors make comparisons without using *like* or *as*. Personification gives human qualities to nonhuman things and ideas. The great power of figurative language is in the enrichment of ideas.

Study the following examples of figures of speech:

- The cat's eyes were like full moons in the darkness. (simile)
- The thief's stare was as cold as ice. (simile)
- The snow was a white blanket over the land. (metaphor)
- The trees fought the storm's winds. (personification)

Notice how the comparison or personification of each example is made. Also notice how the figures of speech help readers visualize the idea expressed by the sentence. Write your own examples of similes, metaphors, and personifications. Ask yourself how the figures of speech enrich the ideas of the sentences. For more practice with figures of speech, do Worksheet 2.20 at the end of this section.

Worksheets

Writing the draft can be the most difficult part of the writing process. The worksheets included in this section are designed to give you practice in the techniques that make writing a draft easier. The skills covered on the worksheets are the foundation of good writing. Try to use these skills in your writing.

The Answer Key offers possible answers to the worksheets.

2.1 Kinds of Sentences

1. Write a declarative sentence using each of the following.

A. puppy _____

_____

B. clouds _____

_____

2. Write an interrogative sentence using each of the following.

A. homework _____

_____

B. lunch _____

_____

3. Write an imperative sentence using each of the following.

A. window _____

_____

B. room _____

_____

4. Write an exclamatory sentence using each of the following.

A. car _____

_____

B. ice _____

_____

Writing the Draft

© Gary Robert Muschla

2.2 Expanding Sentences

1. The dog barked . . . _____

2. Tom slipped . . . _____

3. Brianna almost cried . . . _____

4. The little girl waited . . . _____

5. The thunder rumbled . . . _____

6. Paulo smiled . . . _____

7. Lila practiced . . . _____

8. The river flooded . . . _____

Phrases

the flute each night
inside the house
in pain
when she stubbed her toe
on the icy sidewalk
through the night
for her grandparents to come

because of the heavy rain
during the storm
after dinner
after finishing the test
at the thought of no homework
in relief

2.3 Combining Sentences

Directions: Use *and*, *but*, or *or* to combine and rewrite each pair of sentences.

1. Carl came home from school. He did his homework. _____

_____

2. It snowed all night. School was canceled. _____

_____

3. Susan likes to dance. Staci, her sister, likes to sing. _____

_____

4. The clouds grew darker. The wind began to gust. _____

_____

5. Amanda enjoys basketball. She enjoys softball too. _____

_____

6. It might rain tonight. It might snow. _____

_____

7. Tom could do his math homework. He could work on his science project.

_____

8. The puppy growled at the toy. It was a playful growl. _____

_____

Writing the Draft

© Gary Robert Muschla

2.4 Varying Sentences

Directions: Rewrite each sentence. Use the given word or phrase to vary the form of the sentence. The first one is done as an example.

1. The sun set and daylight faded. (as) _As the sun set, daylight faded._

2. Luis finished his homework and then watched TV. (after) _____

   _____

3. It rained all night, and the river was rising. (because) _____

   _____

4. The computer crashed, and Rashad was almost done with his science

   project. (when) _____

5. Carla had a terrible cold, but she still went to dance practice. (even

   though) _____

6. The rain ended, and the sky quickly cleared. (once) _____

   _____

7. It was raining, and Trish finished reading *Charlotte's Web*. (while) _____

   _____

8. It was the worst part of the storm, and lightning flashed and thunder

   exploded. (during) _____

   _____

Writing the Draft

2.5 Understanding Paragraphs

Directions: Read the article below. It should be written in five paragraphs. Place the symbol └ before the first word that starts each paragraph. Explain your reasons for marking the paragraphs on the lines at the bottom of the page.

Do you know the difference between *meteoroid*, *meteor*, and *meteorite*? Many people find these words confusing. Meteoroids are chunks of rock or metal that speed through space. Some are very large and may be hundreds of feet wide. Others may be the size of a small stone. Most meteoroids orbit the sun. Sometimes a meteoroid will enter the Earth's atmosphere. Friction with the atmosphere will cause it to heat up and burn. When a meteoroid begins to burn in the atmosphere, it leaves a streak of light. This is called a meteor, or shooting star. Most meteors burn up before they hit the ground. If a meteor does not burn completely, it will hit the Earth. A meteor that hits the Earth is called a meteorite. If a meteor is big, this will cause a great explosion and much destruction. Most meteoroids stay safely away from the Earth. Of those that enter the atmosphere, most burn up long before reaching the ground.

_____

_____

_____

_____

_____

_____

_____

_____

2.6 Writing Topic Sentences

Directions: Read each paragraph. Write a topic sentence for each one. Then answer the question at the bottom of the sheet.

1. _____

Although he reads many different kinds of books, Dan likes science fiction the best. He enjoys reading about how people might one day travel to the stars.

2. _____

She stars on her school's soccer, basketball, and softball teams. She also is a fast runner and swimmer. In fact, Jenna is great at every sport she has ever tried.

3. _____

He looked at all the books piled on his desk. His math book, history book, science text, and language arts folder were waiting for him. Bradley didn't know where to begin. But he knew that if he was to finish his homework tonight, he had better start soon.

4. _____

First she looked in the kitchen drawer. That was where she usually put her keys. They weren't there. Next Christy checked her jacket pocket. They weren't there either. Then she searched her room. About to give up, she remembered—her knapsack.

5. Choose one of the paragraphs. Explain what clues helped you to decide on

   the topic sentence. _____

   _____

   _____

   _____

Writing the Draft

127

2.7 Writing Supporting Details

1. Carlita knew there was much to do to get ready for the birthday party.

_____

_____

_____

2. As the storm approached, the sky darkened.

_____

_____

_____

3. Marc enjoyed helping his father around the house.

_____

_____

_____

4. It was the worst heat wave in years.

_____

_____

_____

Writing the Draft

© Gary Robert Muschla

2.8 Showing and Not Telling

1. Sara was a good student. *The first thing Sara did when she got home from school was to begin her homework.*

2. It was a bad storm. _____

_____

3. The puppy was playful. _____

_____

4. Kevin was the winner of the fifth-grade race. _____

_____

5. The winds of the storm were powerful. _____

_____

6. Jess was scared by the strange noises. _____

_____

7. Miguel is an excellent baseball player. _____

_____

8. It snowed heavily. _____

_____

Writing the Draft

2.9 Choosing Adjectives

Directions: Complete each sentence by filling in the blank with an adjective. Use adjectives that help to paint a picture in the reader's imagination. Choose adjectives from the list below. (Not all of the adjectives will be used.)

1. The _____ sun baked the land with heat.

2. Everyone listened as the _____ guide told the _____ story of the ghost wind.

3. Shari looked at the _____ pile of books on her desk.

4. A _____ porch surrounded the _____ house.

5. _____ roses were at the center of the _____ garden.

6. The _____ puppy bounded across the room after the _____ ball.

7. Josh enjoys playing _____ video games.

8. The _____ mountains rose into the _____ sky.

9. As he walked to school, Tim pulled up his collar to block the _____ wind.

10. The wolf's _____ howl filled the _____ woods.

Adjectives

red	tiny	icy	playful	blazing	beautiful
lonely	chilling	blue	old	stately	silly
huge	tall	spongy	exciting	great	empty

2.10 Choosing Adverbs

Directions: Complete each sentence by filling in the blanks with an adverb. Choose adverbs from the list below. (Not all of the adverbs will be used.)

1. The little boy believed the story _____.

2. _____ it would be time to leave.

3. Tara _____ updated her computer with new software.

4. The leaves rustled _____ in the light breeze.

5. Travis studied _____ for the history test.

6. Before giving her speech, Kim practiced it _____.

7. James _____ finishes his homework on time.

8. Not wanting to miss the start of the game, Michael ate his dinner _____.

9. Vanessa likes numbers and finishes her math homework _____.

10. Jon read the directions _____ and got several problems wrong.

Adverbs

recently	often	soon	carelessly	hard
clearly	usually	softly	very	easily
completely	personally	quickly	carefully	loudly

2.11 Writing Descriptions

1. Place or thing: _____

2. Sight words: _____

3. Sound words: _____

4. Touch words: _____

5. Smell words: _____

6. Taste words: _____

7. Paragraph: _____

_____

_____

_____

_____

_____

_____

Writing the Draft

© Gary Robert Muschla

2.12 Understanding the Order of Ideas

1. She could not stop fussing. She took a deep breath and walked toward the piano at the front of the room. Jill was nervous. When her piano instructor called her name, Jill stood. But she still felt nervous. When her mother tried to assure her that she would do fine, Jill smiled. This was her first piano recital, and she was afraid she would make mistakes.

2. He knew it was going to be a busy day. After dinner Alvaro went online to find information for his science report. He came back from practice around four P.M. He watched his little brother until dinner, because his parents went shopping. That morning, he helped his father clean the garage. By the time Alvaro went to sleep that night, he was very tired. In the afternoon Alvaro went to soccer practice. Alvaro woke up early on Saturday.

2.13 Using Active Constructions

1. The ball was hit by Robbie. *Robbie hit the ball.* _____

2. The kite was whipped about by the wind. _____
   _____

3. The dishes were washed by Eduardo. _____
   _____

4. The speech was given by Gina. _____
   _____

5. The cover for the class magazine was designed by Clare. _____
   _____

6. A solo in the fifth-grade concert was sung by Carlos. _____
   _____

7. The bird was sneaked up on by the cat. _____
   _____

8. Dangerous driving conditions were caused by the storm. _____
   _____

Writing the Draft

© Gary Robert Muschla

134

2.14 Using Strong Verbs

1. The fox walked sneakily toward the chicken coop. *The fox crept toward the chicken coop.*

2. The little girl spoke softly during the movie. _____

_____

3. Tommy cried loudly when his toy broke. _____

_____

4. The eagle flew gracefully over the valley. _____

_____

5. Jason moved quickly out of the ball's way. _____

_____

6. Melissa went across the room quietly. _____

_____

Strong Verbs

| whispered | tiptoed | pounced | raced | laughed |
| dodged | soared | crashed | screamed | crept |

Writing the Draft

2.15 Using Verb Tenses Correctly

Directions: Identify whether each of the following sentences is written in the present tense, past tense, or future tense.

1. Liz walked to school with Heather this morning. _____

2. Michael is a good student and a good athlete. _____

3. Alyssa watches her little brother each day after school. _____

4. The magician will be the last act in the show. _____

5. The old dog played like he was still a puppy. _____

6. Roberto will study for his science test after dinner. _____

Directions: Write three sentences of your own. Write one in the present tense, another in the past tense, and the third in the future tense.

1. _____

_____

2. _____

_____

3. _____

_____

Writing the Draft

© Gary Robert Muschla

2.16 Subject-Verb Agreement

Directions: Complete each sentence by writing the correct form of a verb. Choose from the verbs at the bottom of the page. Each verb should be used only once. (Remember to use the correct form.)

1. Tara _____ chocolate ice cream.

2. Wil and Raymondo _____ baseball every day in the summer.

3. Most children _____ playing computer games.

4. Erin _____ her flute every evening.

5. A squirrel _____ in the big tree in our backyard.

6. The Smith twins _____ exactly alike.

7. Tina _____ her little sister with homework.

8. Each day birds _____ to the bird feeder in my yard.

9. The flowers _____ Aunt Janet's garden with color.

10. Antonio _____ hard for every test.

Verbs

play	fill	enjoy	study	help
look	come	like	live	practice

Writing the Draft

2.17 First Person Point of View

Samier sighed, thinking of all the homework he had. He did not know where to begin.

He looked at the pile of books on his desk. He knew he had better start if he wanted to meet his friends later.

Samier opened his math book first. After he finished ten division problems, he did his spelling. Next he did his history.

Finished at last, Samier went to see his friends. They were waiting for him at the basketball court.

As soon as Samier got there, they chose teams and started a game.

_____

_____

_____

_____

_____

_____

_____

_____

_____

_____

_____

2.18 Third Person Point of View

Too excited to sleep, I woke up early. This was the day my father and I were going on a ten-kilometer bike tour. The goal of the tour was to raise money for charity. I thought it would be a great day.

By the time the tour began, I wasn't so sure. The sky had grown dark and a cool wind was blowing. I was worried that it would rain.

All the time we rode, I kept looking at the sky. Just as we came to the finish line, the first drops started to fall on us.

I smiled. It had been a great day after all.

_____

_____

_____

_____

_____

_____

_____

_____

_____

_____

Writing the Draft

2.19 Comparison and Contrast

Directions: Read the article about African elephants and Indian elephants. List how they are alike and different.

The elephant is the largest living land mammal on Earth. There are two species of elephants: the African elephant and the Indian elephant. Both elephants have trunks and eat grass and leaves. But there are important differences, too.

The African elephant is found mostly in the tropical forests and grasslands of Africa. It is the bigger of the two kinds of elephants and can reach a height of thirteen feet. The African elephant also has larger ears. From the top to the bottom, an African elephant's ears may reach a length of five feet.

The Indian elephant is found mostly in India and Southeast Asia. It is usually smaller than the African elephant, but it is taller at the arch of the back.

Compare

How the African elephant and Indian elephant are alike:

_____

_____

_____

_____

Contrast

How the African elephant and Indian elephant are different:

_____

_____

_____

_____

_____

Writing the Draft

2.20 Figures of Speech

1. The hawk soared like a(n) _____ in the sky. _____

2. The moment the race began, Jared ran as fast as a(n) _____ toward the finish line. _____

3. The giant was a(n) _____. _____

4. The burglar sneaked around the house like a(n) _____. _____

5. The shark was a(n) _____ streaking for its target. _____

6. The sound of the smoke detector was a(n) _____ that woke everyone up. _____

Write a sentence that shows personification for each of the following.

7. The sky _____

_____

8. The flowers _____

_____

9. The fireflies _____

_____

Writing the Draft

Revision

R evision is the stage of the writing process where an author reworks and final-izes her ideas. It is a time of "re-seeing" what she has written and making it better.

Revision is necessary to improve writing. It is critical for making writing as clear and meaningful to readers as possible. For most authors, solid revision leads to the successful expression of ideas.

What Is Revision?

In its broadest sense, revision includes any activity that makes a draft better. In its narrowest, it is replacing one word with another because the second word better communicates what the author wants to say. Editing of mechanics—capitalization and punctuation, for example—also occurs during revision. But revision should not be confused with proofreading to correct errors in mechanics (see Part 4, Proofreading).

Revision includes a variety of activities. As you revise your writing, you may do any of the following:

- Rereading
- Rewriting
- Reviewing
- Rethinking
- Rearranging
- Restructuring
- Tightening
- Deleting
- Moving
- Expanding
- Unifying
- Correcting
- Redrafting

Writing is not finished until it has been revised. All professional writers revise their work. During an interview for the *Paris Review*, Ernest Hemingway said that he rewrote the last page of his book *A Farewell to Arms* thirty-nine times before he was satisfied with his work. No one expects you to revise your work like Hemingway, but he illustrates the seriousness with which professional authors revise their work. Professional authors know that their best writing takes form during revision.

Skills in Revision

Revision is detailed, demanding work. Not only must you work to improve specifics—for example, choose the best words to express an idea clearly and smoothly—you must also work to improve the piece as a whole. Each piece is different and has different strengths and weaknesses.

Although just about every article or story benefits from revision, the amount and type of revision vary. Some pieces require a lot of revision. Maybe you drifted off the topic, maybe you did not provide enough information to explain your ideas, or maybe your organization was weak. In other cases, a piece might require only some minor rewriting. During revision, you must recognize what needs to be reworked and what does not.

Being able to recognize what needs to be revised requires an understanding of the fundamentals of good writing (which were discussed in Part 2, Writing the Draft). The following elements are important to any piece and will provide you with direction as you revise your writing.

- Basic structure of opening, body, and closing
- Paragraphs
- Main ideas and details
- Order and sequence
- Varying sentence structure
- Subject-verb agreement
- Active constructions
- Strong verbs
- Showing and not telling
- Consistent tenses
- Consistent point of view
- Figurative language

Revision can be both puzzling and frustrating. It is an individual process, based on your purpose for the piece. Revision is the responsibility of every author.

Plan for Revision

Because revision has so many elements, there can be no set procedure for revising your writing. As you gain experience with revision, you will develop your own methods. But until you master the skills necessary for revision, you will benefit from a basic plan.

Start revising the overall piece and work down to the details. This plan provides direction and helps you to focus on specific elements at different points in the revision process.

Begin by reading through the entire piece and concentrating on unity. In an article that demonstrates unity, all main ideas and supporting details relate to the topic. All parts of the piece are necessary to the whole. Everything moves the piece forward in support of your purpose. For example, an article about how to train a puppy that also includes information about kittens suffers from a lack of unity. It would prove to be confusing to readers, who expect to read about puppies and not kittens. To achieve unity, any material not important to the topic should be deleted.

After making certain that all parts of your writing belong and that the piece shows unity, you should read through the piece again and concentrate on general consistency. Focus on structure, tense, and point of view.

The overall structure of the piece should be logical. There should be a solid opening, logical development through the body, and a strong closing. Main ideas should be supported with details and examples.

All tenses should be consistent. For example, a story should be written in the past tense. An essay might be written in the present. Any unnecessary shifts in tense should be corrected.

Point of view must be consistent as well. If a story is started in the first person point of view, it should continue in the first person. Likewise, if a story is begun in the third person point of view, it should remain in the third person. Switching from first to third person point of view weakens a piece.

Next, focus on paragraphs, sentences, and words. Again, eliminate anything that does not belong. Strive to make sure that paragraphs have a topic sentence and details. Vary and combine sentences, make certain that subjects and verbs agree, use active constructions, and choose the right words to express ideas. Now is the time to make writing the best it can be.

As you gain experience and confidence in revision, you will revise weaknesses as you go along. You will come to see revision as a satisfying part of the writing process, because it helps you to express exactly what you wish to say.

Exercise 3.1 Recognizing Good Writing

Recognizing good writing is a big step toward revising your own writing. Study articles and stories from your texts as examples, and ask yourself why these pieces are good writing. Read the material and note the unity—how everything in the article or story relates to the topic and the author's purpose. Note the organization of the piece and how the structure shows ideas in a logical manner. Note consistent tenses and point of view. See how the author varied his sentences, used active constructions, relied on strong verbs, and achieved a smooth flow of ideas.

Good writing is almost always a result of good revision. Revision is your chance to make your writing as clear and interesting as possible for your readers. It is the time to put ideas into their final shape.

Revision Peer Consultants

One of hardest parts of revision is writing that is not wrong, but that could be improved. I once had a student ask me, "How do you know when to stop revising?" This was an excellent question, for which the only answer is, "When you are convinced the material is as strong and clear as you can make it."

You may find revision to be a hard part of the writing process because you are not sure what to revise. It can be difficult to step far enough back from your writing to see the weaknesses in your material.

Sometimes consulting with a partner can help. You and a partner can read each other's work and offer suggestions for revision. You should not correct each other's papers. Instead you should underline items you feel should be revised and write comments in the margins. The author can then consider revising the places his partner marked. The more practice you have with revision, the more comfortable and confident you will become with the process.

Exercise 3.2 Revision Consultants

Work with a partner on revision. You and your partner are to act as peer revision consultants. You are to read each other's writing and find places where revision could improve the piece. Underline in pencil places on your partners' papers where revision might be helpful. Write brief comments in the margins. For example, a spot where two sentences could be combined might be labeled "Combine sentences." After you and your partner have written and offered comments on each other's piece, discuss the writing. Explain why you think specific instances of his writing should be revised. He then explains why he thinks instances of your writing should be revised. Both of you can then make revisions.

Learning how to revise takes a long time and requires a major effort. These efforts are well worth the undertaking, because revision provides the opportunity to create great writing. It is through revision that you will become a writer.

Worksheets

Revising is a difficult activity. The worksheets included in this section are designed to provide you with practice in revision.

The worksheets, which include both articles and stories, cover a variety of topics. You will find the worksheets challenging in that much of the material that should be revised is not technically wrong, but definitely could be improved. The exceptions are run-on sentences, fragments, unnecessary shifts in tense, faulty point of view, and errors in subject-verb agreement.

The "Guidelines for Revision" (page 148) offer directions for revising. Keep in mind that articles and stories can be revised in different ways, depending on the material and the purpose and outlook of the writer.

The worksheets proceed from relatively basic to more challenging. The directions for Worksheets 3.1 through 3.13 focus on specific elements to revise, while Worksheets 3.14 through 3.25 do not provide any hints of what weaknesses to look for. Each worksheet has several items that could be revised. Because revised articles and stories will vary, the Answer Key offers a possible revision of each worksheet.

Always work hard to revise your writing. It is through revision that you will achieve your best writing.

Guidelines for Revision

Asking yourself the following questions can help you revise your writing.

1. Is my topic focused?

2. Do all of my ideas and details relate to my topic?

3. Does my writing have an opening, body, and closing?

4. Have I used paragraphs?

5. Does each paragraph have a main idea? Have I supported each main idea with details?

6. Have I used correct order and sequence?

7. Have I varied my sentence construction?

8. Have I used active constructions?

9. Have I used strong verbs?

10. Do my subjects and verbs agree?

11. Did I show and not tell?

12. Are my tenses consistent?

13. Is my point of view consistent?

14. Have I deleted all unnecessary information and words?

15. Have I expressed my ideas clearly?

Revision

3.1 The Moon

Directions: Revise the article. Make any changes you feel will improve it. Be sure it has an opening, body, and closing. (The revised article should have three paragraphs.) Eliminate any unnecessary information. Rewrite the revised article on a separate sheet of paper.

The moon is the Earth's natural satellite. About 240,000 miles away, it is our closest neighbor in space. Many people look at the moon each night. It is the only body in the solar system people have visited. The moon is barren. The moon is lifeless. The moon is a dangerous world. It has no atmosphere. It has no liquid water. The surface is covered with dust and craters. Scientists believe the craters were caused by meteorites crashing into the moon millions of years ago. Other planets have moons, too. In the shade, the temperature on the moon can be as cold as −280° Fahrenheit. In sunlight, the temperature can be as hot as 260° Fahrenheit. Scientists have learned much about the moon. They continue to study the moon. They hope that by learning more about the moon they will learn more about our solar system.

Revision

3.2 Geysers

A geyser is a natural hot spring. It shoots water and steam high into the air. Most geysers are found in three parts of the world. These three parts of the world are the western United States, Iceland, and New Zealand. Geysers occur when hot volcanic rock heats underground water to high temperatures. The water is heated. It begins to boil. It is becoming hotter and hotter. Steam forms and forces the water upward through cracks in the rock. There is enough pressure sometimes to shoot the hot water and steam into the air. The most famous geyser in the world is Old Faithful in Yellowstone National Park. This geyser, Old Faithful, erupts on average once every ninety-four minutes each day. Between 3,700 and 8,400 gallons of hot water shoot up to 170 feet in the air. Watching a geyser is exciting. It is very thrilling. Geysers are one of nature's thrilling shows.

3.3 The Beginnings of Roller Coasters

Directions: Revise the article. Make any changes you feel will improve it. Be sure it has an opening, body, and closing. (The revised article should have four paragraphs.) Eliminate any unnecessary information. Rewrite the revised article on a separate sheet of paper.

Modern roller coasters have their beginnings with Russian ice slides. Millions of people love roller coasters. The slides were first built in the mid-1600s. The ice slides were big structures. Some were between seventy and eighty feet high. During winter the slides were enjoyed by a lot of people. They were built of wood. They were covered with thick ice. Large sleds sped down the slide along an icy path for hundreds of feet. The builders even constructed stairs for riders to walk up the slides. Some historians believe the Russians also built the first true roller coaster in the late 1700s. It was a carriage with wheels. It was built in St. Petersburg. From these simple beginnings, we have the super roller coasters of today. A person can only imagine what future coasters will be like.

Revision

3.4 Healthy Teeth

Having healthy teeth is important. Strong, healthy teeth help you to chew your food properly. Healthy teeth, they help you to speak clearly. Healthy teeth help you to look your best. It is very important to have healthy teeth.

To keep your teeth healthy, you must keep them clean. This is very, very important. Brush your teeth at least twice each day. You should brush them after breakfast and before bed. You should visit your dentist twice each year. The dentist will check for cavities and clean your teeth. Brush for at least three minutes. Be sure to brush in the back and along the sides of your teeth. You should clean your teeth with dental floss. The floss, which you should use every day, will clean places your toothbrush cannot reach.

Strong, clean teeth will help to keep you healthy. They, your strong, clean teeth, are something to smile about.

Revision

3.5 The Importance of Exercise

Directions: Revise the article. Make any changes you feel will improve it. Especially pay attention to subject-verb agreement and varying sentence structure. Rewrite the revised article on a separate sheet of paper.

Exercising each day will help to keep you in good health. It will also help you think better. It will help you sleep better. It will help you feel better.

Exercise help your body stay fit. It causes you to breathe more deeply. It makes your heart pump more strongly. It makes your muscles work harder. It makes your body use more calories. It helps to keep your body at a healthy weight.

You can exercise in many ways. You can walk. You can run. You can jog. You can play sports. You can ride your bike. You can skate. You can swim. You can dance. Any activity that make your heart beat faster is good.

Exercise is important for your health. You should try to exercise every day.

Revision

3.6 The Wandering Albatross

Directions: Revise the article. Make any changes you feel will improve it. Especially pay attention to unity, sentence structure, and subject-verb agreement. Eliminate any unnecessary information. Rewrite the revised article on a separate sheet of paper.

The wandering albatross is a large seabird. When it spreads it wings. The wings measure up to twelve feet from tip to tip. This is the largest wingspread of any living bird.

There are many kinds of albatrosses. Along with the wandering albatross. There is the black-footed albatross, the royal albatross, and the sooty albatross. There are even more. The wandering albatross is found over the oceans of the Southern Hemisphere.

Wandering albatrosses does not have a permanent home. They spend most of their lives flying over the oceans of the Southern Hemisphere. They feed on small fish. They can sleep on the sea's surface. When they become tired of flying. Like most seabirds, they drink seawater. They land only to mate, they make their nests on empty islands.

Because of its size, the wandering albatross have few predators. Most wandering albatrosses have long lives. The wandering albatross is thought to be one of the few birds to die of old age.

Revision

3.7 Doomed City

Pompeii was a city in ancient Italy. It was built a few miles south of Mt. Vesuvius. Mt. Vesuvius is an active volcano. Pompeii was a wealthy city. Pompeii was always busy with trade.

The day of August 24 in the year A.D. 79 began like any other. Without warning. The top of Vesuvius exploded. Great clouds of smoke and ash rose high into the sky. Soon the light of the sun was blocked. The sky became dark.

People awoke that day and began their chores. In the distance the volcano sent lazy dark smoke into the sky. But this was normal. No one was worried.

Scientists study volcanoes. They hope to learn how to predict when a volcano will erupt.

The eruption continued throughout the day and night. The city was covered with ash and molten rock, it is estimated that two thousand people died. The doomed city of Pompeii disappeared in a day.

Revision

3.8 The Oregon Trail

Directions: Revise the article. Make any changes you feel will improve it. Especially pay attention to sentence structure and active constructions. Rewrite the revised article on a separate sheet of paper.

The Oregon Trail was the most important pioneer route to the American Northwest. The trail was about two thousand miles long. It started in Independence, Missouri, it ended at the Columbia River in Oregon.

The journey over the trail was long. It was hard. It was dangerous, too. The trip could take as long as six months. Many hardships were faced by the pioneers. Terrible storms, illness, lack of food, and attacks by Native Americans were constant threats. Sometimes as many as half of the people of a wagon train died on the trail.

Despite the hardships. The trail was followed by thousands of pioneers. They believed that the Oregon Trail was a way to a new life.

Revision

3.9 Laura Ingalls Wilder

Directions: Revise the article. Make any changes you feel will improve it. Especially pay attention to sentence structure and active constructions. Rewrite the revised article on a separate sheet of paper.

Laura Ingalls was born in Pepin, Wisconsin, on February 7, 1867. Laura Ingalls was the second daughter of Charles and Caroline Ingalls.

During her childhood, Laura traveled westward with her family in a covered wagon. Wisconsin, Kansas, and Minnesota were crossed by the Ingalls family, the Dakota Territory was where they finally settled.

Laura loved living on the prairie. Life could be hard. It was full of joy. Laura enjoyed helping her parents with the chores.

Laura grew up. She married Almanzo Wilder. Laura and Almanzo moved to Mansfield, Missouri. A home there was built by Laura and Almanzo.

Her family's pioneer days were remembered fondly by Laura. She would tell stories about living on the prairie to Rose, her daughter. Rose, her daughter, suggested that her mother write the stories down so that others could read them. These stories became the Little House series.

Revision

3.10 Moving In

Directions: Revise the story. Make any changes you feel will improve it. Especially pay attention to varying sentence structure and verb tenses. Rewrite the revised story on a separate sheet of paper.

Rachel stood in her new room. Boxes are everywhere. The room was bigger than her room in her old house. The room in her old house was small. The new room did not feel like home.

Rachel missed her old house. She missed her old friends. She is worried about making new friends.

Rachel unpacked a few boxes. She went outside. She sat on the front steps. She looked around the yard. There were flowers and trees. The yard was pretty.

Rachel noticed a girl from the house across the street walking toward her. The girl is about Rachel's age.

"Hi, I'm Danielle," the girl says. "But my friends call me Dani. . . ."

3.11 The Messy Room

Directions: Revise the story. Make any changes you feel will improve it. Especially pay attention to varying sentence structure, strong verbs, and descriptions. Rewrite the revised story on a separate sheet of paper.

Jason was in his room. It was messy. He was upset.

He could not find his science report. He had finished it yesterday. He finished it right after school. Then he had gone out to play with his friends.

He looked at his messy desk. His mother was always urging him to be neater. He went through the stuff on it. He went through the drawers in the desk. They were messy, too. He searched his messy dresser. He searched under his messy bed.

He tried to remember where he put the report. Suddenly he remembered.

He picked up his knapsack. It was in a folder. He had put it in the knapsack yesterday so that he would not lose it.

Jason heard the school bus. He picked up his knapsack. He went to the door.

Revision

3.12 The Monster Coaster

Maria stood in front of the big roller coaster. Carlos, her younger brother, was with her.

It was called the Monster. Maria had been looking forward to riding it for weeks. But now she is not sure she wants to.

It was so high. It was so fast. And it had three loops. Maria likes fast rides, but this one scares her.

"Come on, Maria," says Carlos. "Let's get in line." He takes my hand and started pulling me.

At first Maria does not move. It was as if my feet will not go.

"Maria, come on," said Carlos. "You're not afraid, are you?"

Maria smiled weakly. If her little brother was not afraid, I should not be afraid either.

"Let's go," Maria says. She led Carlos to the line.

3.13 The Game

Directions: Revise the story. Make any changes you feel will improve it. Especially pay attention to point of view and descriptions. Rewrite the revised story on a separate sheet of paper.

One second was left in the championship game between the Hawks and Cougars. The score was 38 to 38.

Kevin Williams, the Cougars' youngest player, was at the foul line. If he made either of his two foul shots, the Cougars would be champions. But Kevin was not a good foul shooter.

The referee gave him the ball.

I took a deep breath. I bounced the ball to calm myself.

I looked up at the basket. I aimed and let it go. It missed. The home crowd sounded sad.

The referee handed Kevin the ball again. Once more I bounced the ball to steady myself. I aimed and let it go.

I watched it go through the net.

Revision

3.14 The Sun

Directions: Revise the article. Make any changes you feel will improve it. Rewrite the revised article on a separate sheet of paper.

The sun is a star. Like other stars, it is a giant ball of burning gases. It is made up mostly of hydrogen. This is a gas. The sun is about 93 million miles from Earth. This is very, very far. Earth is one of the nine planets that orbit the sun. Inside the sun, hydrogen atoms are fused (forced together) to make helium. Great amounts of energy are produced. Some of this energy reaches the Earth. As light and heat. The temperature on the surface of the sun is about 11,000° Fahrenheit. Inside the sun, near the center, the temperature is about 35 million degrees Fahrenheit. The sun makes life possible on the Earth. Without the sun, the Earth would be a cold, dark planet. It would be lifeless.

Revision

3.15 The Bear Facts

Directions: Revise the article. Make any changes you feel will improve it. Rewrite the revised article on a separate sheet of paper.

Bears are large mammals. There are several kinds of bears. Black bears were once found throughout North America. Now they are found mostly in wilderness areas. Black bears are one of the smallest bears, they weigh between two hundred and four hundred pounds. Grizzly bears are among the most dangerous bears. They can weigh up to one thousand pounds. Other animals are hunted by grizzlies for food. Grizzlies may be brown, black, or cream-colored. The fur on their shoulders and backs is often tipped with white. This gives them a "grizzled" look. Polar bears are found on the islands of the Arctic Ocean. They are big bears. Polar bears may be ten feet tall and weigh up to fifteen hundred pounds. Seals, young walruses, and fish are hunted by polar bears. Their thick white coats keep them warm in icy temperatures. Bears are found in many parts of the world. Bears are among nature's most interesting animals.

Revision

3.16 Smokey Bear

Directions: Revise the article. Make any changes you feel will improve it. Rewrite the revised article on a separate sheet of paper.

Many people have heard of Smokey Bear. They know Smokey is a symbol for fire prevention. Not everyone knows the story of the real Smokey.

On a spring day in 1950, parts of New Mexico were burned by a terrible fire. A baby black bear was found in a tree by firefighters. The men gently took the cub from the tree, they did not know what to do with him. A rancher who had been helping the firefighters offered to take the injured cub home. The cub had climbed the tree to try to escape the flames. But his paws and back were burned.

A forest ranger heard about the cub. He drove to the ranch. Had the injured cub flown to Santa Fe. His injuries were treated by a veterinarian there.

Eventually the cub was sent to Washington, D.C. He was given a home in the National Zoo. The cub became known as Smokey Bear.

3.17 Johnny Appleseed

Directions: Revise the article. Make any changes you feel will improve it. Rewrite the revised article on a separate sheet of paper.

Johnny Appleseed was a real man. His name was John Chapman, he was born in 1774 in Leominster, Massachusetts.

Settlers moved westward. John went with them. For nearly fifty years. John planted apple trees. He planted apple trees in what became the states of Ohio, Michigan, Illinois, and Indiana. People called John the Apple Tree Man or Johnny Appleseed.

John worked alone. He walked across the wilderness. He would find a good spot for planting. He would clear the land. He would plant apple seeds. He would build a brush fence around the spot to keep animals out. An orchard would fill the spot.

John Chapman died in 1845. The apple orchards he left behind were a gift to the settlers who came after him.

Revision

3.18 The Ice

Directions: Revise the story. Make any changes you feel will improve it. Rewrite the revised story on a separate sheet of paper.

With very, very nervous fingers Tamara tightened the laces of her ice skates. She took a deep breath.

"Don't worry," her coach said. "You'll do fine."

That made Tamara worry even more. That was what people told her last winter. Tamara remembered. Trying to jump and turn in the air for the first time. The awful, terrible pain of her ankle breaking would never be forgotten by Tamara. Her ankle hurt really, really badly for days. Her slow recovery took months.

Tamara started skating again a few weeks ago. She had not tried to jump and spin, she would today.

Tamara stood and stepped onto the ice, her heart was thumping.

"Good luck," was said by her coach.

Tamara nodded.

She skated around the rink. She tried to build up her courage.

She began to skate faster and faster. She lifted off the ice. She rose and spun.

She landed perfectly!

Revision

3.19 Giant Squid

When ancient sailors reported seeing sea monsters. They might have seen a giant squid. The giant squid is a frightening animal. It is a scary animal, too.

The name *giant squid* fits this creature. The giant squid can grow to be 150 feet long. The giant squid's big eyes can be 3 feet across. The giant squid has long tentacles. The giant squid's prey is caught with its tentacles.

The giant squid is one of the fastest creatures in the ocean. It can draw water into its body. It can then force the water out. That shoots the animal forward like a rocket.

Giant squid live deep in the ocean. They live far below the surface of the ocean. Sometimes they come to the surface. This creature could have been mistaken for a sea monster by ancient sailors.

Revision

3.20 The Earl of Sandwich

Directions: Revise the article. Make any changes you feel will improve it. Rewrite the revised article on a separate sheet of paper.

John Montagu is a nobleman. He lived in England in the 1700s. He is the fourth Earl of Sandwich. He was also a well-known gambler.

When he was gambling. He would sit at the table for hours. One day he is gambling. He gets hungry. But he did not want to leave the game. So he sends a servant to bring him meat between two slices of bread.

Other gamblers think this is a good idea. They got hungry. They said something like, "I'll have what Sandwich had." Soon the name Sandwich came to mean meat between two slices of bread.

The sandwich was named after the Earl of Sandwich in 1762. Since then countless sandwiches have been made.

3.21 Little Dinosaurs

Directions: Revise the article. Make any changes you feel will improve it. Rewrite the revised article on a separate sheet of paper.

When most people think of dinosaurs. They think of big creatures. But there are little dinosaurs too.

The smallest dinosaur is thought to be a microraptor. This dinosaur was about sixteen inches long. This dinosaur was about the size of a crow.

Saltopus was a little bigger. Than a microraptor. It was about two feet long. It was the size of a small cat. It walks on two legs. It has a long head. It has dozens of sharp teeth.

Compsognathus was about the size of a big chicken. It was about three feet long. It has two thin legs. It has three-toed feet. It had a long tail. It had a pointed head, had sharp teeth.

Even smaller dinosaurs may be discovered by scientists someday. But most people will probably continue to think of dinosaurs as big creatures.

Revision

3.22 An Early Flyer

Directions: Revise the article. Make any changes you feel will improve it. Rewrite the revised article on a separate sheet of paper.

Wiley Post was born in Grand Plain, Texas, in 1899. He did not have much formal schooling. He became one of the most famous early pilots.

In 1931, Post and his navigator flew around the world. His navigator was Harold Charles Gatty. They made the flight in eight days, fifteen hours, and fifty-one minutes. A world record was set by them.

Two years later, in 1933, it was decided by Post to fly around the world by himself. He set a new record of seven days, eighteen hours, and forty-nine minutes.

Wiley Post died on August 15, 1935. His plane crashed at Point Barrow, Alaska. He was called a national hero.

3.23 A Busy Day

Directions: Revise the story. Make any changes you feel will improve it. Rewrite the revised story on a separate sheet of paper.

Kareem woke up early on Saturday. He had a busy day planned.

After breakfast, Kareem went to soccer practice. He was the goalie for his team, he liked soccer.

After lunch, Kareem helped his father in the yard. They raked leaves. They trimmed the hedges. His father mowed the lawn. Kareem weeded the flower beds. They worked in the yard all afternoon.

In the evening, Kareem's friends came. His friends' names were David and Charles. The boys decided to watch a movie. After the movie was done, his friends went home. Kareem watched TV a little while with his parents.

He soon went to bed. It had been a busy day. He was tired.

Revision

3.24 Platypus

Directions: Revise the article. Make any changes you feel will improve it. Rewrite the revised article on a separate sheet of paper.

The platypus is a very strange, unusual animal. It is a mammal. It also has traits of a duck. Another name for this very strange, unusual animal is the duckbill.

Platypuses are found in Australia. They live in burrows along the banks of rivers. They make their homes near water.

An adult platypus is about fourteen inches in length. It has a long body. It has a flat tail. It uses its flat tail for swimming.

The platypus have many traits of mammals. It is warm-blooded, it has fur, it feeds its young milk.

But the platypus also have some traits of ducks. Instead of a nose and mouth. The platypus has a leathery bill. It has webbed feet for swimming. Like a duck, it lays eggs. A baby platypus hatches from an egg.

The platypus is truly a very strange, unusual animal.

Revision

3.25 The Myth of Daedalus and Icarus

Directions: Revise the story. Make any changes you feel will improve it. Rewrite the revised story on a separate sheet of paper.

Daedalus and his son Icarus were imprisoned on the island of Crete. In hopes of escaping. A very dangerous and very daring plan was thought of by Daedalus. He would build wings of wax and feathers. For Icarus and himself.

Daedalus begins his work. When the day came that the wings were done, he calls to Icarus. He warns Icarus not to fly too close to the sun. The heat would melt the wax. The wings would fall apart.

Icarus promises his father he would be careful. But once they set off. The boy is overcome with the thrill of flying like a bird.

Daedalus sees his son flying higher and higher. He called to him that he was too close to the sun. Yet the boy keeps going higher.

Soon the wax on Icarus's wings begins to melt. Feathers started to fall off. The boy flapped the wings wildly. But the wings came apart, he fell into the sea and drowned.

Revision

Proofreading

Proofreading is the part of the writing process that puts the final polish on a piece. Proofreading should not be done until writing has been revised. It is a time when you catch and correct any last errors in punctuation, capitalization, spelling, and word usage.

Proofreading is just as demanding as the other stages of writing. While it is true that most errors have been corrected by this time, the errors that remain often are easy to miss. By now you may have become so close to the piece that mistakes are hard to find. If you have done a good job of revision, proofreading is much like looking for a needle in the haystack.

For just about every piece, no matter how careful a writer was during revision, a few mistakes remain. Proofreading requires concentration and a good eye.

Proofreading Strategies

Proofreading is different from ordinary reading. In ordinary reading, the average reader focuses on a few words at a time and moves quickly through the line. This is usually enough for the reader to gain an understanding of the material. Proofreading, though, requires that the proofreader read and examine every word and punctuation mark.

When done properly, proofreading is slow, hard work. Anything less will miss a few of those last mistakes.

Exercise 4.1 A Proofreading Plan

Proofreading is the last step before finishing writing. Here are general guidelines for proofreading:

1. Read slowly and concentrate on punctuation, capitalization, spelling, and word usage.

2. Look at the page to make sure paragraphs are fully indented, margins are correct, and there are no gaps in spacing.
3. Proofread the piece two or three times. It is likely that each time you will find a few more minor errors. Only when no more errors are found is proofreading done.

Choose an example of your work to proofread. This might be a previously completed piece or a piece that you have just finished. Proofread the piece with care and concentration.

Follow the suggestions above whenever proofreading your work. With practice and experience, you will eventually develop your own methods for proofreading.

Proofreading and Computer Screens

Computers have made the work of most writers easier. The capabilities of the machines for writing and revising are without question. But proofreading on a computer screen can cause problems for writers.

Reading text on a computer screen can be trying to the eyes. Some writers tend to read material less carefully than they do printed text on paper. In addition, text on paper has a different "look" from text on a screen. When authors read text on paper, most are more likely to concentrate and examine words and punctuation with greater care.

Of course, some writers do quite well proofing on a computer screen. You may eventually fall into this category. Growing up with computers will help you be comfortable in writing, revising, and proofreading written material on a screen.

Exercise 4.2 Proofreading on a Screen

Following are guidelines for proofreading on a computer screen:

1. Read slowly and carefully. [Most people tend to read faster on a computer screen than a printed page.]
2. Use the cursor arrow to go through the text one line at a time.
3. Read every word of each line before going to the next line.
4. Concentrate on every piece of punctuation.
5. Use the print preview to check the page for paragraphs, skipped spaces, and unnecessary returns.

Proofread a finished piece on a computer screen for practice. If you are not comfortable proofing on a computer screen, print the material and proof the printed text.

The Value of Proofreading Partners

Because writers often have trouble viewing their writing objectively, proofreading can be difficult for them. They may pass over small errors that others quickly see. A proofreading partner can help find many of the minor errors that the writer may overlook.

Proofreading partners can help each other become better writers. During proofreading students should underline any errors they find in their partner's work. An alternative to marking clean pages is to use stick-on notes. If partners cannot agree whether an item is wrong, they should consult an appropriate reference book. Having a dictionary and grammar book handy is helpful when proofreading.

Exercise 4.3 Partners for Proofing

Work with a partner or friend. Proofread each other's writing. Find any remaining errors in punctuation, capitalization, spelling, or word usage. Underline any mistakes you find in pencil, or use stick-on notes. After proofreading, discuss the mistakes you found in your partner's writing. Your partner then discusses the mistakes he found in your work. Check reference sources if necessary. Correct any mistakes and produce the final copy.

Proofreading is not a task of writing to be taken lightly. It is the final stage of the writing process, before sharing your writing with readers.

Worksheets

Proofreading is a challenging task. The worksheets in this section are designed to provide you with practice in proofreading.

The worksheets, which include both articles and stories, cover a variety of topics. Errors appear in punctuation, capitalization, and word usage. The "Guidelines for Proofreading" (page 178) offer direction for your proofreading efforts.

The worksheets in this part proceed from relatively basic—for example, focusing on end punctuation, commas, and capitalization—to more challenging. Along with general errors in punctuation and capitalization, the directions for Worksheets 4.1 through 4.15 focus on specific errors. The worksheets average about ten errors each, some a few less and some a few more. Many of the errors are obvious. Some are tricky and require sharp concentration.

The Answer Key for the worksheets is found on page 205. Note: While most of the corrections are clear-cut, a few, especially concerning the use of commas, are open to interpretation of the context.

As you gain experience with proofreading, your proofreading skills will grow. Proofreading will help you to present polished writing to your readers.

Guidelines for Proofreading

1. Sentences begin with capital letters.

2. Sentences end with correct punctuation.

3. Paragraphs are indented.

4. Proper nouns and proper adjectives are capitalized.

5. Commas are used correctly (between the items in a list, to connect compound sentences, and after introductory words, phrases, and clauses).

6. Apostrophes are used correctly (with possessive nouns and contractions).

7. Pronouns are used correctly.

8. Quotation marks are used correctly (for dialogue and for the titles of short stories, articles, poems, and songs).

9. Italics and underlining are used correctly (for the titles of books, the names of newspapers and magazines, and the titles of movies).

10. Words are used correctly (especially homophones such as *there, their,* and *they're; your* and *you're; its* and *it's;* and *to, too,* and *two*).

Proofreading

© Gary Robert Muschla

4.1 The Gila Monster

Directions: Proofread and correct the article. Pay close attention to errors in ending punctuation, commas, and capitalization. Make your corrections on this sheet.

The Gila monster is not a monster. It is a lizard. It is the largest lizard in the United States. it is also the only poisonous lizard in our Country

The Gila monster is found in the Desert areas of Arizona Nevada, Utah, and new Mexico. It is named after the Gila river.

An adult Gila monster is easy to recognize. It is about two feet long and weighs between three and five pounds. It has a thick body, and short legs. Its black, scaly body is covered with orange pink and yellow spots.

The poison of a Gila monster is usually not strong enough to kill Humans. But the bite of the lizard, is painful.

Proofreading

4.2 How to Study for Tests

Do you know how to study for tests. Here are some suggestions.

On the days leading up to the Test, listen to any reviews your teacher gives. This will help you find out what may be on the Test. You will be able to study the right material. If you have any questions about the material, ask your teacher?

Begin studying a day or two before the Test go over your notes and key parts of your textbook. Do not wait until the last minute, to study. Students who study ahead of time usually do better than those who cram.

On the day of the Test be confident. people who study do better than people who do not study.

4.3 The Family Picnic

Directions: Proofread and correct the story. Pay close attention to errors in ending punctuation, commas, and capitalization. Make your corrections on this sheet.

Katie woke up early on saturday! She was too excited to sleep! Today was the day of her family's picnic.

Each year the Morgan Family met at Ellis park for a picnic. All of Katie's aunts uncles and cousins would be there.

After breakfast Katie helped her mother pack food in coolers. They packed, sandwiches, salads, and desserts.

The drive to the park seemed to take forever As they entered the park, Katie's father headed for lake Ellis where the Picnic Grounds were located. Nearing the lake, Katie saw that people were already there.

She smiled. This, would be a great day.

Proofreading

4.4 Frogs and Toads

Directions: Proofread and correct the article. Pay close attention to errors in ending punctuation, commas, and capitalization. Make your corrections on this sheet.

Frogs and Toads are amphibians. They are animals that can live both in water and on land. Although frogs and toads are much alike they are different too. Do you know how they are different.

Frogs spend much of their lives in water. Their bodies are usually slimmer than the bodies of toads they have smooth skin and they have long legs for jumping.

Toads spend most of their lives on land. Their bodies are usually thicker than the bodies of frogs they have warty skin and they have shorter back legs.

Of course for most People these are not very big differences. To them frogs and toads are more alike than different.

Proofreading

4.5 Why Plants and Animals Become Extinct

Throughout history many plants and animals have become extinct. these plants and animals are no longer alive anywhere on our planet. Plants, and animals become extinct for many reasons.

Big changes in Climate can cause plants and animals to become extinct. If the climate of an area that once got much rain becomes very dry, some plants and animals may die out?

Sometimes people change the land where plants, and animals live For example, people cut down Forests. They may use wood to build houses or they may clear land for farming. The plants and animals that lived there may die.

Overhunting can cause animals to become extinct. Before the settlers came, buffalo ranged across the american Great Plains. By the end of the nineteenth century buffaloes were hunted almost to extinction.

Every effort should be made to protect plants and animals from extinction. Once a plant, or animal, becomes extinct it is too late.

Proofreading

4.6 The Test

Directions: Proofread and correct the story. Pay close attention to errors in punctuation and capitalization. Especially pay attention to the use of commas and apostrophes. Make your corrections on this sheet.

Marissa went down the hall toward her classroom. She felt foolish coming back to school. But she had forgotten her history book. without her history book, she wouldnt be able to study for the big history test Tomorrow.

History was a hard subject for Marissa. If she wanted a high grade on her report card she had to study.

Just before she got to the classroom she saw a paper on the floor. When she picked the paper up, her eyes widened. It was the tests answer key.

This was her chance to get a good grade. She held the key for a long moment.

That would be cheating and Marissa wasn't a cheater.

She went into her classroom. Her teacher ms. Carter was there. Marissa went to the desk and handed the key to ms. Carter.

4.7 Deserts

Directions: Proofread and correct the article. Pay close attention to errors in punctuation and capitalization. Especially pay attention to the use of commas and apostrophes. Make your corrections on this sheet.

With it's oceans lakes, and rivers, the Earth has plenty of water. But not all parts of the Earth have a lot of water. about one-fifth of the Earth's land is desert.

Desert's are dry areas of land. Some deserts get only an inch or two of rainfall every year.

Although it is hard for life to survive in deserts many plants and animals make the desert their home. Plants such as the Cactus live in deserts. Animals such as Snakes, Lizards, and Camels live in deserts too.

People also live in or near deserts. Many of these people believe that deserts have a special beauty. This beauty, is found nowhere else on our planet.

Proofreading

4.8 Earthquakes

Directions: Proofread and correct the article. Pay close attention to errors in punctuation and capitalization. Especially pay attention to the use of commas and apostrophes. Make your corrections on this sheet.

Earthquakes are more common than most people think. Thousands of earthquakes occur each year but most are so weak they aren't felt. Only about one out of five hundred earthquakes causes damage

In the past, people didnt know what caused earthquakes? Today scientists' know that the Earth's crust, it's outer layer is divided into great pieces. These pieces called plates are made of Rock. The plates move slowly in different directions. They may move past each other away from each other or toward each other. Sometimes a long crack, called a fault, forms between plates. If enough stress builds up along a fault an earthquake occurs.

Minor earthquakes cause little damage. Major quakes can destroy buildings bridges and roads. They can cause thousands of deaths.

Proofreading

4.9 The Race

Directions: Proofread and correct the story. Pay close attention to errors in punctuation and capitalization. Especially pay attention to the use of commas, apostrophes, and quotation marks. Make your corrections on this sheet.

It was Field Day at Manuels School. As he waited for his turn to run Manuel was worried. He was the fastest boy in the fifth grade but that could change today.

Mr. Wilkins, Manuels teacher called the last four boys to the starting line.

Manuel stepped forward. This was a race against time. Whoever ran the fastest would be the fastest runner in the fifth grade?

Manuel took a deep breath, and bent his legs. Every muscle was ready. He looked at the finish line at the end of the field. Another teacher Ms Edwards was there with a stopwatch.

"On your mark! said Mr. Wilkins. Get set! Go!"

The boys began. Manuel took powerful strides. he heard kids cheering but his thoughts were only on running. He was pulling ahead.

Manuel crossed the line first.

Sixteen point three seconds ms. Edwards said!

Manuel smiled That was the best time of the day. He was still the fastest runner in the fifth grade.

Proofreading

4.10 A Business Letter

123 Mountain road

High Point WA 00000

September 25 2010

Mr William Connors, Circulation Manager

Rugged Outdoors Magazine

50 Carter street

Centerville, CA 00000

Dear Mr. Connors,

I would like to subscribe to "Rugged Outdoors Magazine." Enclosed is a

check for $19.95 for a subscription for one year.

Thank you.

Yours Truly.

Jon Petersen

Jon Petersen

4.11 Best Friends

Directions: Proofread and correct the article. Pay close attention to errors in punctuation and capitalization. Especially pay attention to the use of apostrophes and pronouns. Make your corrections on this sheet.

Me and Jimmy are best friends. We've been best friends since kindergarten. Some kids think its strange that a girl and a boy in fifth grade are best friends. But Jimmy and me have a lot in common.

We live next door to each other. We both like sports we like the same type of music, and we like the same kinds of Movies. But most important, we just like hanging out together. Jimmys easy to talk to and he's always willing to help when i have a problem. I do the same for him.

No matter what happens I know I can count on Jimmy. I suppose thats whats best about being best friends.

Proofreading

4.12 Arbor Day

Arbor Day is a day for planting trees. All fifty States in the US. celebrate Arbor Day.

Julius Sterling Morton 1832–1902 founded the first Arbor Day in Nebraska on April 10 1872. Morton believed that Nebraskas Land could be improved by the planting of trees.

Nebraskas first Arbor Day was a great success! People planted more than one million trees. A second Arbor Day took place in 1884 and also was successful. In 1885, Nebraska made Arbor Day a holiday and set April 22nd to celebrate it. April 22nd was Julius Sterling Mortons birthday.

In the following years, other states set aside there own Arbor Days. Although the dates vary because of climate, Arbor Day remains a day for planting trees. It is a day people throughout the Country can celebrate our environment.

4.13 Play Ball!

Directions: Proofread and correct the story. Pay close attention to errors in punctuation and capitalization. Especially pay attention to quotation marks, apostrophes, and pronouns. Make your corrections on this sheet.

Jason looked at the darkening sky. He turned to Martin his friend.

"I bet its going to rain" Jason said.

"It'll hold off until after the game, said Martin."

The two boys had just arrived at the baseball field. Some of the players of both teams were already their. This was the first game of the season and all the boys were excited.

Coach Smith instructed the boys to begin warm-ups.

Jason and Martin took their places with there teammates and began stretching.

Jason looked back at the sky. He loved baseball and had been looking forward to this first game for weeks.

You worry too much," said Martin. From the looks of those clouds, it wont rain for a while."

"I hope you're right," said Jason.

A little while later the game was ready to start.

"Play Ball!" the umpire called.

"See," said Martin. "You worry too much."

Jason smiled. "Maybe your right."

Proofreading

4.14 Reading

Directions: Proofread and correct the article. Pay close attention to errors in punctuation and capitalization. Especially pay attention to the use of quotation marks and italics. Make your corrections on this sheet.

Everybody in my family likes to read. Books, magazines, and newspapers are everywhere in our home.

My father reads the newspaper every morning. He reads the "New York Times" on the train to work. He also reads magazines. His favorite is *Newsweek*.

My mother likes to read novels. She reads a new novel every week. She likes Mysteries the best.

Stephie my sister likes short stories and poems. One of her favorite short stories is *The Open Window* by H. H. Munro. Her favorite poem is Robert Frost's "The Road Not Taken."

I like to read novels. My favorites are science fiction. If I had to pick one favorite, I would choose "A wrinkle in Time" by Madeleine L' Engle.

Proofreading

4.15 The Big Slope

Directions: Proofread and correct the story. Pay close attention to errors in punctuation and capitalization. Especially pay attention to the use of quotation marks, apostrophes, and word usage. Make your corrections on this sheet.

Kyra stood on the top of the Mountain. She looked down the ski slope. Breakneck Trail disappeared in the distance. She took a deep breath too steady herself.

"Dont be afraid," said Mia her big sister. "You can make it down."

"Im not worried about making it down, said Kyra. She forced a smile. "I'm worried about how many pieces I'll be in."

Mia patted her on the shoulder. "You don't have to do this, she said."

"Yes, I do" said Kyra. "This is the only trail on this mountain Ive never gone down."

Mia smiled. "Keep you're knees bent, she said, and remember to lean into the turns."

"Wish me luck," Kyra said. She pushed off with her poles and started down the trail.

As she picked up speed she heard Mias voice behind her.

"Good luck."

Proofreading

4.16 Sound

What causes sound. The sounds of a crying baby, the slamming of a door or the roar of a jets engines are all produced in the same way.

Sound is caused by vibrations. When something vibrates it moves back and forth rapidly. Imagine pulling a string on a Guitar. As the string vibrates, it makes a sound.

Vibrating objects cause the molecules in the air around them to move. As the molecules move the vibrations travel, through the air in waves. When these waves reach your ear, you hair the sound.

As sound waves move away from a vibrating object they become weaker. A sound becomes fainter the farther away you are from its source.

Proofreading

4.17 Checkers

Have you ever played checkers? If you have you have played one of the Worlds oldest games.

Games similar to checkers were played by the ancient egyptians about thirty-five hundred years ago. A form of the game was also played in ancient Greece. the modern form of checkers appeared about five hundred years ago.

Checkers is a game of skill. Two players' play against each other. Each player has twelve playing pieces on a board that has sixty-four squares. the goal of the game is to capture an opponents pieces. The best players' think ahead and take advantage of there opponent's mistakes.

Checkers is played around the world. Minor rules vary somewhat from country to country but the basic game is the same.

Proofreading

4.18 Safety First

Directions: Proofread and correct the article. Pay close attention to errors in punctuation, capitalization, and word usage. Make your corrections on this sheet.

Most accidents happen at home. Although nobody can prevent every accident you can prevent many accidents by being careful and using common sense.

Many accidents occur in the kitchen. always be careful around a stove so that you don't get burned. Don't leave paper towels napkins, or cloths near the stove. Handle knives with care. Dont touch their sharp blades and always cut away from your body. Keep knives in a safe place wear young children cant get them.

Many accidents also occur in the bathroom. Never use electrical Appliances such as a hear dryer near water. Use a rubber mat to prevent anyone from slipping in the bathtub. keeping soap in a soap dish will help prevent people from slipping on it.

Accidents can happen to anyone: But using common sense and being careful can reduce the chances of an accident happening to you.

Proofreading

4.19 Whale-Watching

Directions: Proofread and correct the story. Pay close attention to errors in punctuation, capitalization, and word usage. Make your corrections on this sheet.

Hallie took her seat in the boat. She was not pleased. Her parents and her were spending one of there vacation days looking for whales. her mom called it whale-watching. Hallie would have liked to spend the day at the lake, where her parents had rented a cabin for the weak.

"This will be exciting Hallies mother said.

"I'd rather be swimming at the lake Hallie said."

"You can swim every day for the rest of the week said her father. "But you can't see a whale every day."

Hallie didnt understand what could be so great about seeing a whale. She pulled up the hood of her Sweatshirt to block the cool breeze.

It was early afternoon when one of the boats crewmen pointed ahead.

"There! he cried.

Hallie turned and saw a fantastic creature rise from the water.

"Its beautiful," she said, and she forgot all about swimming.

197

4.20 Colors

Directions: Proofread and correct the article. Pay close attention to errors in punctuation, capitalization, and word usage. Make your corrections on this sheet.

Colors make the world a brighter place. Imagine how dull the World would be without colors?

Colors can be divided into three kinds primary, secondary, and intermediate.

The primary colors are red yellow and blue. These are known as the basic colors. They cant be made bye mixing any other colors.

The secondary colors are orange green, and violet. Secondary colors are made by mixing to primary colors. Mixing red and yellow makes orange. Mixing yellow and blue makes green. Mixing blue and red makes violet.

Intermediate colors are made by mixing primary and secondary colors. Mixing white, or black with colors will make them lighter or darker.

It is remarkable that all colors are based on combinations of red, yellow, and blue. What a colorful world, the Earth is!

4.21 Sasha, Come Down

I was doing my homework when Annie my little sister came running into my room.

"Cassie come quick!" she cried.

"What's wrong," I said.

"Its Sasha! Annie said between sobs. She's stuck in a big tree." Sasha was our cat.

I followed her downstairs and out the front door.

I looked up at the big oak tree in our yard. Sure enough Sasha was sitting on a high branch. Although she had climbed up she was afraid to climb down.

"Sasha, come down," I said. But all I received was a sad meow.

Their wasn't anything I could do except to keep calling Sasha to come down. But the cat wouldnt budge.

Fortunately, my father and mother soon came home from work. My father got the Ladder from the Garage and got Sasha.

I smiled as annie scolded the silly cat.

"Sasha don't ever do that again," she said.

Proofreading

4.22 Rainbows

Directions: Proofread and correct the article. Pay close attention to errors in punctuation, capitalization, and word usage. Make your corrections on this sheet.

When sunlight strikes water droplets in the air a rainbow may form. The rainbow makes an arc in the sky. Sometimes its ends seem to touch the Earth.

Why does a rainbow appear when sunlight hits water droplets. The answer lies in sunlight. a ray of sunlight contains all the colors of the spectrum, red, orange, yellow, green, blue, and violet. Tiny water droplets separate the sunlight into it's different colors. Under the right conditions that creates a rainbow.

Rainbows most often are seen near the end of a rain shower. But they can also be seen in the spray of a waterfall a fountain or a garden hose.

According two Legend a pot of gold is at the end of a rainbow. Of course no one can ever reach the end of a rainbow. As you approach a rainbow, it seems to move farther a way and soon disappears.

4.23 Babysitting

Directions: Proofread and correct the story. Pay close attention to errors in punctuation, capitalization, and word usage. Make your corrections on this sheet.

Lateesha rang the doorbell to the home of Mr. and Mrs Morgan. This was the first time she was to babysit for there son Nathan. She hoped Nathan, who was only five years old would behave. Her friend Christina had babysat for Nathan once, and she would never do it again.

Mrs. Morgan opened the door with a big smile.

Lateesha saw Nathan standing in the living room. He was smiling to. He seemed like a nice boy.

After Mrs. Morgan gave Lateesha instructions, her and her husband got ready to leave.

"Remember Lateesha," mrs. Morgan said at the door, Nathan must be in bed by nine."

"I won't forget." Lateesha said.

For the next two hours she read to Nathan, they colored, and they watched TV. Nathan was so delightful that Lateesha began to wonder if Christina had babysat four the same boy.

At nine o'clock Lateesha announced that it was time for bed.

Nathan looked at her and smiled.

"No!" he said. The firmness in his voice told Lateesha that it was going to bee a long night.

Proofreading

4.24 Summer Challenge

It was tennis day at summer camp. Darci was to play Lora in the championship Match.

Darci looked at Lora and frowned. She doubted that she could beat Lora.

"Loras a great player," Darci said to Melissa her best friend.

"She is," said Melissa, "But she loses her cool. She tries to hit the ball as hard as she can every time. She hits a lot of balls out of bounds. Then she gets mad and hits them even harder. That makes her miss more."

"But how does that help me," said Darci. "I'll be lucky to return half of her shots."

"You have to play a steady game, said Melissa. "Don't make mistakes. Thats how your going to beat her."

"You mean she'll beat herself," said Darci.

Melissa nodded.

Not long after the match began Darci new her friend was right. When the match was finished Darci was the tennis champ.

4.25 Travelers

Directions: Proofread and correct the story. Pay close attention to errors in punctuation, capitalization, and word usage. Make your corrections on this sheet.

Captain Danos watched the main viewing screen on the bridge of his Spaceship. The tiny world grew on the screen. As it became larger oceans and land masses appeared threw patchy white clouds.

"It looks much like home" said Danos to Lieutenant Tarka.

"Yes it does." Tarka said.

"Does the planet have intelligent life," Danos asked?

Tarka checked some instruments.

"I think it does." he said. "I'm picking up radio transmissions."

"Are the inhabitants advanced enough for us to make contact," said Danos.

"Doubtful," Tarka said. "They seem primitive and warlike."

"Too bad," said Danos. "Whats the name of they're planet."

"Earth," said Tarka.

Captain Danos gave the order to pass bye Earth.

Proofreading

Answer Key

Part 1
Answers for the worksheets throughout this section will vary, depending on your responses.

Part 2

2.1 Sentences will vary.

2.2 Answers may vary. Possible answers follow. 1. The dog barked through the night. 2. Tom slipped on the icy sidewalk. 3. Brianna almost cried when she stubbed her toe. 4. The little girl waited for her grandparents to come. 5. The thunder rumbled during the storm. 6. Paulo smiled at the thought of no homework. 7. Lila practiced the flute each night. 8. The river flooded because of the heavy rain.

2.3 Answers may vary. Possible answers follow. 1. Carl came home from school and did his homework. 2. It snowed all night, and school was canceled. 3. Susan likes to dance, but Staci, her sister, likes to sing. 4. The clouds grew darker, and the wind began to gust. 5. Amanda enjoys basketball, but she enjoys softball too. 6. It might rain tonight, or it might snow. 7. Tom could do his math homework, or he could work on his science project. 8. The puppy growled at the toy, but it was a playful growl.

2.4 Answers may vary. Possible answers follow. 2. After Luis finished his homework, he watched TV. 3. Because it rained all night, the river was rising. 4. When the computer crashed, Rashad was almost done with his science project. 5. Even though Carla had a terrible cold, she still went to dance practice. 6. Once the rain ended, the sky quickly cleared. 7. While it was raining, Trish finished reading *Char-*

lotte's Web. 8. During the worst part of the storm, lightning flashed and thunder exploded.

2.5 └Do you know the difference between *meteoroid*, *meteor*, and *meteorite*? Many people find these words confusing. └Meteoroids are chunks of rock or metal that speed through space. Some are very large and may be hundreds of feet wide. Others may be the size of a small stone. Most meteoroids orbit the sun. └Sometimes a meteoroid will enter the Earth's atmosphere. Friction with the atmosphere will cause it to heat up and burn. When a meteoroid begins to burn in the atmosphere, it leaves a streak of light. This is called a meteor, or shooting star. Most meteors burn up before they hit the ground. If a meteor does not burn completely, it will hit the Earth. A meteor that hits the Earth is called a meteorite. └If a meteor is big, this will cause a great explosion and much destruction. └Most meteoroids stay safely away from the Earth. Of those that enter the atmosphere, most burn up long before reaching the ground.

2.6 Answers may vary. Possible answers follow. 1. Dan likes to read. 2. Jenna is an excellent athlete. 3. Bradley had a lot of homework. 4. Christy couldn't find her keys. 5. Clues will vary.

2.7 Answers may vary. Possible answers follow. 1. She needed to clean the house, set up decorations, set the table, and get the cake. 2. The wind picked up. Thunder could be heard in the distance. The first drops of rain began to fall. 3. He helped in the yard. He painted the fence. He washed the car. 4. The temperature was in the nineties. Everyone was hot. The land baked in the heat.

2.8 Answers may vary. Possible answers follow. 2. The storm ripped the big oak tree from the ground. 3. The puppy chased the ball. 4. Kevin dashed across the finish line ahead of the other fifth graders. 5. The winds of the storm shook the house. 6. Jess jumped at the strange noises. 7. Miguel blasted the ball over the fence. 8. It was impossible to see through the heavy, falling snow.

2.9 Answers may vary. Possible answers follow. 1. blazing 2. old; chilling 3. huge 4. great; stately 5. Red; beautiful 6. playful; spongy 7. exciting 8. tall; blue 9. icy 10. lonely; empty

2.10 Answers may vary. Possible answers follow. 1. completely 2. Soon 3. recently 4. softly 5. hard 6. often 7. usually 8. quickly 9. easily 10. carelessly

2.11 Answers may vary.

2.12 1. Jill was nervous. She could not stop fussing. This was her first piano recital, and she was afraid she would make mistakes. When her mother tried to assure her that she would do fine, Jill smiled. But she still felt nervous. When her piano instructor called her name, Jill stood. She took a deep breath and walked toward the piano at the front of the room. 2. Alvaro woke up early on Saturday. He knew it was going to be a busy day. That morning, he helped his father clean the garage. In the afternoon Alvaro went to soccer practice. He came back from practice around four P.M. He watched his little brother until dinner because his parents went shopping. After dinner Alvaro went online to find information for his science report. By the time Alvaro went to sleep that night, he was very tired.

2.13 2. The wind whipped the kite about. 3. Eduardo washed the dishes. 4. Gina gave the speech. 5. Clare designed the cover for the class magazine. 6. Carlos sang a solo in the fifth-grade concert. 7. The cat sneaked up on the bird. 8. The storm caused dangerous driving conditions.

2.14 Answers may vary. Possible answers follow. 2. The little girl whispered during the movie. 3. Tommy screamed when his toy broke. 4. The eagle soared over the valley. 5. Jason dodged the ball. 6. Melissa tiptoed across the room.

2.15 1. past 2. present 3. present 4. future 5. past 6. future

2.16 1. likes 2. play 3. enjoy 4. practices 5. lives 6. look 7. helps 8. come 9. fill 10. studies

2.17 I sighed, thinking of all the homework I had. I did not know where to begin.

I looked at the pile of books on my desk. I knew I had better start if I wanted to meet my friends later.

I opened my math book first. After I finished ten division problems, I did my spelling. Next I did my history.

Finished at last, I went to see my friends. They were waiting for me at the basketball court.

As soon as I got there, we chose teams and started a game.

2.18 Stories may vary, depending on the name of the point-of-view character.

Too excited to sleep, Deanna woke up early. This was the day her father and she were going on a ten-kilometer bike tour. The goal of the tour was to raise money for charity. Deanna thought it would be a great day.

By the time the tour began, she wasn't so sure. The sky had grown dark and a cool wind was blowing. She was worried that it would rain.

All the time they rode, Deanna kept looking at the sky. Just as they came to the finish line, the first drops started to fall on them.

Deanna smiled. It had been a great day after all.

2.19 Compare: Both elephants have trunks and eat grass and leaves. Contrast: African elephants are found mostly in Africa. The African elephant is larger and has bigger ears. Indian elephants are found mostly in India and Southeast Asia. Indian elephants are taller at the arch of the back.

2.20 Answers may vary. Possible answers follow. 1. plane, S 2. rabbit, S 3. monster, M 4. fox, S 5. torpedo, M 6. scream, M

Part 3
Revised articles and stories will vary. Possible revisions are provided.

3.1 The moon is the Earth's natural satellite. About 240,000 miles away, it is our closest neighbor in space. It is the only body in the solar system people have visited.

The moon is a barren, lifeless, and dangerous world. It has no atmosphere and no liquid water. The surface is covered with dust and craters. In the shade, the temperature on the moon can be as cold as −280° Fahrenheit. In sunlight, the temperature can be as hot as 260° Fahrenheit.

Scientists continue to study the moon. They hope that by learning more about the moon they will learn more about our solar system.

3.2 A geyser is a natural hot spring that shoots water and steam high into the air. Most geysers are found in the western United States, Iceland, and New Zealand.

Geysers occur when hot volcanic rock heats underground water to high temperatures. As the water is heated, it begins to boil. Steam forms and forces the water upward through cracks in the rock. Sometimes there is enough pressure to shoot the hot water and steam into the air.

The most famous geyser in the world is Old Faithful in Yellowstone National Park. Old Faithful erupts on average once every ninety-four minutes each day. Between 3,700 and 8,400 gallons of hot water shoot up to 170 feet in the air.

Watching a geyser is exciting. Geysers are one of nature's thrilling shows.

3.3 Modern roller coasters have their beginnings with Russian ice slides. The slides were first built in the mid-1600s.

The ice slides were big, wooden structures. Some were between seventy and eighty feet high. They were covered with thick ice. Large sleds sped down the slide along an icy path for hundreds of feet. The builders even constructed stairs for riders to walk up the slides.

Some historians believe the Russians also built the first true roller coaster in the late 1700s in St. Petersburg. It was a carriage with wheels.

From these simple beginnings, we have the super roller coasters of today. A person can only imagine what future coasters will be like.

3.4 Having healthy teeth is important. Strong, healthy teeth help you to chew your food properly. They help you to speak clearly and look your best.

To keep your teeth healthy, you must keep them clean. Brush your teeth at least twice each day, after breakfast and before bed. Brush for at least three minutes. Be sure to brush in the back and along the sides of your teeth. You should also clean your teeth with dental floss. The floss will clean places your toothbrush cannot reach. Finally, visit your dentist twice each year. The dentist will check for cavities and clean your teeth.

Strong, clean teeth will help to keep you healthy. Your teeth are something to smile about.

3.5 Exercising each day will help to keep you in good health. It will also help you think better, sleep better, and feel better.

Exercise helps your body stay fit. It causes you to breathe more deeply and makes your heart pump more strongly. It makes your muscles work harder and makes your body use more calories. Exercise helps to keep your body at a healthy weight.

You can exercise in many ways. You can walk, run, or jog. You can play sports. You can ride your bike. You can skate, swim, or dance. Any activity that makes your heart beat faster is good.

Exercise is important for your health. You should try to exercise every day.

3.6 The wandering albatross is a large seabird. When it spreads it wings, the wings measure up to twelve feet from tip to tip. This is the largest wingspread of any living bird.

Wandering albatrosses do not have a permanent home. They spend most of their lives flying over the oceans of the Southern Hemisphere, where they feed on small fish. They can sleep on the sea's surface when they become tired of flying. Like most seabirds, they drink seawater. They land on empty islands only to mate and make their nests.

Because of its size, the wandering albatross has few predators. The wandering albatross is thought to be one of the few birds to die of old age.

3.7 Pompeii was a city in ancient Italy. It was built a few miles south of Mt. Vesuvius, an active volcano. Pompeii was a wealthy city and was always busy with trade.

The day of August 24 in the year A.D. 79 began like any other. People awoke that day and began their chores. In the distance the volcano sent lazy dark smoke into the sky. But this was normal. No one was worried.

Without warning, the top of Vesuvius exploded. Great clouds of smoke and ash rose high into the sky. Soon the light of the sun was blocked and the sky became dark.

The eruption continued throughout the day and night. The city was covered with ash and molten rock. It is estimated that two thousand people died. The doomed city of Pompeii disappeared in a day.

3.8 The Oregon Trail was the most important pioneer route to the American Northwest. The trail was about two thousand miles long. It started in Independence, Missouri, and ended at the Columbia River in Oregon.

The journey over the trail was long, hard, and dangerous. The trip could take as long as six months. The pioneers faced many hardships. Terrible storms, illness, lack of food, and attacks by Native Americans were constant threats. Sometimes as many as half of the people of a wagon train died on the trail.

Despite the hardships, thousands of pioneers followed the trail. They believed that the Oregon Trail was a way to a new life.

3.9 Laura Ingalls was born in Pepin, Wisconsin, on February 7, 1867. She was the second daughter of Charles and Caroline Ingalls.

During her childhood, Laura traveled westward with her family in a covered wagon. The Ingalls family crossed Wisconsin, Kansas, and Minnesota. They finally settled in the Dakota Territory.

Laura loved living on the prairie. Life could be hard, but it was full of joy too. Laura enjoyed helping her parents with the chores.

When Laura grew up, she married Almanzo Wilder. Laura and Almanzo moved to Mansfield, Missouri, and built a home.

Laura remembered her family's pioneer days fondly. She would tell Rose, her daughter, stories about living on the prairie. Rose suggested that her mother write the stories down so that others could read them. These stories became the Little House series.

3.10 Rachel stood in her new room. Boxes were everywhere. The room was bigger than the room in her old house. But it did not feel like home.

Rachel missed her old house. She missed her old friends and was worried about making new friends.

After unpacking some boxes, Rachel went outside. She sat on the front steps. She looked around the pretty yard that was filled with colorful flowers and trees.

She noticed a girl from the house across the street walking toward her. The girl was about her own age.

"Hi, I'm Danielle," the girl said. "But my friends call me Dani. . . ."

3.11 Jason stood in his messy room. He was upset.

He could not find his science report. He had finished it yesterday right after school. Then he had gone out to play with his friends.

He looked at his messy desk. First he searched through the books and papers on it. Next he searched the messy drawers in the desk. Then he searched his messy dresser. Finally, he searched under his messy bed.

He tried to remember where he put the report. Suddenly, he remembered.

He picked up his knapsack. The report was in a folder. He had put it in the knapsack yesterday so that he would not lose it.

Jason heard the school bus. He grabbed his knapsack and hurried to the door.

3.12 Maria stood in front of the big roller coaster. Carlos, her younger brother, was with her.

The roller coaster was called the Monster. Maria had been looking forward to riding it for weeks, but now she was not sure.

The Monster was high and fast, and had three loops. Maria liked fast rides, but this one scared her.

"Come on, Maria," said Carlos. "Let's get in line." He took her hand and started pulling her.

At first Maria did not move. It was as if her feet would not go.

"Maria, come on," said Carlos. "You're not afraid, are you?"

Maria smiled weakly. If her little brother was not afraid, she should not be afraid either.

"Let's go," Maria said. She led Carlos to the line.

3.13 One second was left in the championship game between the Hawks and Cougars. The score was 38 to 38.

Kevin Williams, the Cougars' youngest player, was at the foul line. If he made either of his two foul shots, the Cougars would be champions. But Kevin was not a good foul shooter.

The referee gave him the ball.

He took a deep breath and bounced the ball to calm himself.

He looked up at the basket, aimed, and let the ball go. It bounced off the rim. The home crowd groaned.

The referee handed Kevin the ball again. Once more he bounced the ball to steady himself. He aimed and let it go.

He watched the ball fall perfectly through the net.

3.14 The sun is a star. Like other stars, it is a giant ball of burning gases. It is made up mostly of hydrogen.

Inside the sun, hydrogen atoms are fused (forced together) to make helium. Great amounts of energy are produced. Some of this energy reaches the Earth as light and heat. The temperature on the surface of the sun is about 11,000° Fahrenheit. Inside the sun, near the center, the temperature is about 35 million degrees Fahrenheit.

The sun makes life possible on the Earth. Without the sun, the Earth would be a cold, dark, lifeless planet.

3.15 Bears are large mammals. There are several kinds of bears.

Black bears were once found throughout North America, but now they are found mostly in wilderness areas. Black bears are one of the smallest bears. They weigh between two hundred and four hundred pounds.

Grizzly bears are among the most dangerous bears and can weigh up to one thousand pounds. Grizzlies hunt other animals for food. Grizzlies may be brown, black, or cream-colored. The fur on their shoulders and backs is often tipped with white. This gives them a "grizzled" look.

Polar bears are found on the islands of the Arctic Ocean. They may be ten feet tall and weigh up to fifteen hundred pounds. Polar bears hunt seals, young walruses, and fish. Their thick white coats keep them warm in icy temperatures.

Bears are found in many parts of the world. They are among nature's most interesting animals.

3.16 Many people have heard of Smokey Bear. They know Smokey is a symbol for fire prevention, but not everyone knows the story of the real Smokey.

On a spring day in 1950, a terrible fire burned parts of New Mexico. Firefighters found a baby black bear in a tree. The cub had climbed the tree to try to escape the flames. But his paws and back were burned. The men gently took the cub from the tree. They did not know what to do with him. A rancher who had been helping the firefighters offered to take the injured cub home.

A forest ranger heard about the cub. He drove to the ranch and had the injured cub flown to Santa Fe. A veterinarian there treated his injuries.

Eventually the cub was sent to Washington, D.C., and was given a home in the National Zoo. The cub became known as Smokey Bear.

3.17 Johnny Appleseed was a real man. His name was John Chapman. He was born in 1774 in Leominster, Massachusetts.

When settlers moved westward, John went with them. For nearly fifty years John planted apple trees in what became the states of Ohio, Michigan, Illinois, and Indiana. People called John the Apple Tree Man or Johnny Appleseed.

John worked alone. As he walked across the wilderness, he would find a good spot for planting. He would clear the land and plant apple seeds. He would build a brush fence around the spot to keep animals out. In time, an orchard would fill the spot.

John Chapman died in 1845. The apple orchards he left behind were a gift to the settlers who came after him.

3.18 With nervous fingers Tamara tightened the laces of her ice skates. She took a deep breath.

"Don't worry," her coach said. "You'll do fine."

That made Tamara worry even more. That was what people told her last winter. Tamara remembered trying to jump and turn in the air for the first time. She would never forget the terrible pain of her ankle breaking. Her ankle hurt badly for days, and her slow recovery took months.

Tamara started skating again a few weeks ago. She had not tried to jump and spin, but she would today.

Tamara stood and stepped onto the ice. Her heart was thumping.

"Good luck," said her coach.

Tamara nodded.

She skated around the rink and tried to build up her courage.

She began to skate faster and faster. She lifted off the ice, rose, and spun.

She landed perfectly!

3.19 When ancient sailors reported seeing sea monsters, they might have seen a giant squid. The giant squid is a frightening animal.

The name *giant squid* fits this creature. The giant squid can grow to be 150 feet long. Its big eyes can be 3 feet across. It has long tentacles that it uses to catch prey.

The giant squid is one of the fastest creatures in the ocean. It can draw water into its body and force the water out. That shoots the animal forward like a rocket.

Giant squid live deep in the ocean, but sometimes they come to the surface. If ancient sailors saw a giant squid on the surface, they could have mistaken it for a sea monster.

3.20 John Montagu was a nobleman who lived in England in the 1700s. He was the fourth Earl of Sandwich and a well-known gambler.

When he was gambling, he would sit at the table for hours. One day he was gambling and got hungry. But he did not want to leave the game. He sent a servant to bring him meat between two slices of bread.

Other gamblers thought this was a good idea. When they got hungry, they said something like, "I'll have what Sandwich had." Soon the name Sandwich came to mean meat between two slices of bread.

The sandwich was named after the Earl of Sandwich in 1762. Since then, countless sandwiches have been made.

3.21 When most people think of dinosaurs, they think of big creatures. But there were little dinosaurs too.

The smallest dinosaur is thought to be a microraptor. This dinosaur was about sixteen inches long and was about the size of a crow.

Saltopus was a little bigger than a microraptor. It was about two feet long, the size of a small cat. It walked on two legs, had a long head, and had dozens of sharp teeth.

Compsognathus was about the size of a big chicken. It was about three feet long. It had two thin legs, three-toed feet, and a long tail. It had a pointed head and sharp teeth.

Scientists may discover even smaller dinosaurs someday. But most people will probably continue to think of dinosaurs as big creatures.

3.22 Wiley Post was born in Grand Plain, Texas, in 1899. Although he did not have much formal schooling, he became one of the most famous early pilots.

In 1931, Post and his navigator, Harold Charles Gatty, flew around the world. They made the flight in eight days, fifteen hours, and fifty-one minutes. They set a new world record.

In 1933, Post decided to fly around the world by himself. He set a new record of seven days, eighteen hours, and forty-nine minutes.

Wiley Post died on August 15, 1935. His plane crashed at Point Barrow, Alaska. He was called a national hero.

3.23 Kareem woke up early on Saturday. He had a busy day planned.

After breakfast, Kareem went to soccer practice. He liked soccer and was the goalie for his team.

After lunch, Kareem helped his father in the yard. They raked leaves and trimmed the hedges. As his father mowed the lawn, Kareem weeded the flower beds. They worked in the yard all afternoon.

In the evening, Kareem's friends, David and Charles, came. The boys decided to watch a movie. After his friends went home, Kareem watched TV a little while with his parents.

Tired, he soon went to bed. It had been a busy day.

3.24 The platypus is a strange, unusual animal. It is a mammal, but it also has traits of a duck. Another name for the platypus is the duckbill.

Platypuses are found in Australia. They live in burrows along the banks of rivers.

An adult platypus is about fourteen inches in length. It has a long body and a flat tail. It uses its tail for swimming.

The platypus has many traits of mammals. It is warm-blooded, has fur, and feeds its young milk.

But the platypus also has some traits of ducks. Instead of a nose and mouth, the platypus has a leathery bill. It has webbed feet for swimming, and it lays eggs. A baby platypus hatches from an egg.

The platypus is truly a strange, unusual animal.

3.25 Daedalus and his son Icarus were imprisoned on the island of Crete. In hopes of escaping, Daedalus thought of a dangerous and daring plan. He would build wings of wax and feathers for Icarus and himself.

Daedalus began his work. When the day came that the wings were done, he called to Icarus. He warned Icarus not to fly too close to the sun. The heat would melt the wax and the wings would fall apart.

Icarus promised his father he would be careful. But once they set off, the boy was overcome with the thrill of flying like a bird.

Daedalus saw his son flying higher and higher. He called to him that he was too close to the sun. Yet the boy kept going higher.

Soon the wax on Icarus's wings began to melt. Feathers started to fall off. The boy flapped the wings wildly, but the wings came apart. Icarus fell into the sea and drowned.

Part 4

In a few articles and stories, corrections may vary depending on context. This is particularly true in the case of commas. Corrected articles and stories follow.

4.1 The Gila monster is not a monster. It is a lizard. It is the largest lizard in the United States. It is also the only poisonous lizard in our country.

The Gila monster is found in the desert areas of Arizona, Nevada, Utah, and New Mexico. It is named after the Gila River.

An adult Gila monster is easy to recognize. It is about two feet long and weighs between three and five pounds. It has a thick body and short legs. Its black, scaly body is covered with orange, pink, and yellow spots.

The poison of a Gila monster is usually not strong enough to kill humans. But the bite of the lizard is painful.

4.2 Do you know how to study for tests? Here are some suggestions.

On the days leading up to the test, listen to any reviews your teacher gives. This will help you find out what may be on the test. You will be able to study the right material. If you have any questions about the material, ask your teacher.

Begin studying a day or two before the test. Go over your notes and key parts of your textbook. Do not wait until the last minute to study. Students who study ahead of time usually do better than those who cram.

On the day of the test be confident. People who study do better than people who do not study.

4.3 Katie woke up early on Saturday. She was too excited to sleep. Today was the day of her family's picnic.

Each year the Morgan family met at Ellis Park for a picnic. All of Katie's aunts, uncles, and cousins would be there.

After breakfast Katie helped her mother pack food in coolers. They packed sandwiches, salads, and desserts.

The drive to the park seemed to take forever. As they entered the park, Katie's father headed for Lake Ellis, where the picnic grounds were located. Nearing the lake, Katie saw that people were already there.

She smiled. This would be a great day.

4.4 Frogs and toads are amphibians. They are animals that can live both in water and on land. Although frogs and toads are much alike, they are different too. Do you know how they are different?

Frogs spend much of their lives in water. Their bodies are usually slimmer than the bodies of toads, they have smooth skin, and they have long legs for jumping.

Toads spend most of their lives on land. Their bodies are usually thicker than the bodies of frogs, they have warty skin, and they have shorter back legs.

Of course, for most people these are not very big differences. To them, frogs and toads are more alike than different.

4.5 Throughout history many plants and animals have become extinct. These plants and animals are no longer alive anywhere on our planet. Plants and animals become extinct for many reasons.

Big changes in climate can cause plants and animals to become extinct. If the climate of an area that once got much rain becomes very dry, some plants and animals may die out.

Sometimes people change the land where plants and animals live. For example, people cut down forests. They may use wood to build houses, or they may clear land for farming. The plants and animals that lived there may die.

Overhunting can cause animals to become extinct. Before the settlers came, buffaloes ranged across the American Great Plains. By the end of the nineteenth century buffaloes were hunted almost to extinction.

Every effort should be made to protect plants and animals from extinction. Once a plant or animal becomes extinct, it is too late.

4.6 Marissa went down the hall toward her classroom. She felt foolish coming back to school. But she had forgotten her history book. Without her history book, she wouldn't be able to study for the big history test tomorrow.

History was a hard subject for Marissa. If she wanted a high grade on her report card, she had to study.

Just before she got to the classroom, she saw a paper on the floor. When she picked the paper up, her eyes widened. It was the test's answer key.

This was her chance to get a good grade. She held the key for a long moment.

That would be cheating, and Marissa wasn't a cheater.

She went into her classroom. Her teacher, Ms. Carter, was there. Marissa went to the desk and handed the key to Ms. Carter.

4.7 With its oceans, lakes, and rivers, the Earth has plenty of water. But not all parts of the Earth have a lot of water. About one-fifth of the Earth's land is desert.

Deserts are dry areas of land. Some deserts get only an inch or two of rainfall every year.

Although it is hard for life to survive in deserts, many plants and animals make the desert their home. Plants such as the cactus live in deserts. Animals such as snakes, lizards, and camels live in deserts too.

People also live in or near deserts. Many of these people believe that deserts have a special beauty. This beauty is found nowhere else on our planet.

4.8 Earthquakes are more common than most people think. Thousands of earthquakes occur each year, but most are so weak they aren't felt. Only about one out of five hundred earthquakes causes damage.

In the past, people didn't know what caused earthquakes. Today scientists know that the Earth's crust, its outer layer, is divided into great pieces. These pieces, called *plates*, are made of rock. The plates move slowly in different directions. They may move past each other, away from each other, or toward each other. Sometimes a long crack, called a fault, forms between plates. If enough stress builds up along a fault, an earthquake occurs.

Minor earthquakes cause little damage. Major quakes can destroy buildings, bridges, and roads. They can cause thousands of deaths.

4.9 It was field day at Manuel's school. As he waited for his turn to run, Manuel was worried. He was the fastest boy in the fifth grade, but that could change today.

Mr. Wilkins, Manuel's teacher, called the last four boys to the starting line.

Manuel stepped forward. This was a race against time. Whoever ran the fastest would be the fastest runner in the fifth grade.

Manuel took a deep breath and bent his legs. Every muscle was ready. He looked at the finish line at the end of the field. Another teacher, Ms. Edwards, was there with a stopwatch.

"On your mark!" said Mr. Wilkins. "Get set! Go!"

The boys began. Manuel took powerful strides. He heard the other kids cheering, but his thoughts were only on running. He was pulling ahead.

Manuel crossed the line first.

"Sixteen point three seconds!" Ms. Edwards said.

Manuel smiled. That was the best time of the day. He was still the fastest runner in the fifth grade.

4.10
123 Mountain Road
High Point, WA 00000
September 25, 2010

Mr. William Connors, Circulation Manager
Rugged Outdoors Magazine
50 Carter Street
Centerville, CA 00000

Dear Mr. Connors:

I would like to subscribe to *Rugged Outdoors Magazine*. Enclosed is a check for $19.95 for a subscription for one year.

Thank you.

Yours truly,
Jon Petersen

4.11 Jimmy and I are best friends. We've been best friends since kindergarten.

Some kids think it's strange that a girl and a boy in fifth grade are best friends. But Jimmy and I have a lot in common.

We live next door to each other. We both like sports, we like the same type of music, and we like the same kinds of movies. But most important, we just like hanging out together. Jimmy's easy to talk to, and he's always willing to help when I have a problem. I do the same for him.

No matter what happens, I know I can count on Jimmy. I suppose that's what's best about being best friends.

4.12 Arbor Day is a day for planting trees. All fifty states in the U.S. celebrate Arbor Day.

Julius Sterling Morton (1832–1902) founded the first Arbor Day in Nebraska on April 10, 1872. Morton believed that Nebraska's land could be improved by the planting of trees.

Nebraska's first Arbor Day was a great success. People planted more than one million trees. A second Arbor Day took place in 1884 and also was successful. In 1885, Nebraska made Arbor Day a holiday and set April 22nd to celebrate it. April 22nd was Julius Sterling Morton's birthday.

In the following years, other states set aside their own Arbor Days. Although the dates vary because of climate, Arbor Day remains a day for planting trees. It is a day people throughout the country can celebrate our environment.

4.13 Jason looked at the darkening sky. He turned to Martin, his friend.

"I bet it's going to rain," Jason said.

"It'll hold off until after the game," said Martin.

The two boys had just arrived at the baseball field. Some of the players of both teams were already there. This was the first game of the season, and all the boys were excited.

Coach Smith instructed the boys to begin warm-ups.

Jason and Martin took their places with their teammates and began stretching.

Jason looked back at the sky. He loved baseball and had been looking forward to this first game for weeks.

"You worry too much," said Martin. "From the looks of those clouds, it won't rain for a while."

"I hope you're right," said Jason.

A little while later the game was ready to start.

"Play ball!" the umpire called.

"See," said Martin. "You worry too much."

Jason smiled. "Maybe you're right."

4.14 Everybody in my family likes to read. Books, magazines, and newspapers are everywhere in our home.

My father reads the newspaper every morning. He reads the *New York Times* on the train to work. He also reads magazines. His favorite is *Newsweek*.

My mother likes to read novels. She reads a new novel every week. She likes mysteries the best.

Stephie, my sister, likes short stories and poems. One of her favorite short stories is "The Open Window" by H. H. Munro. Her favorite poem is Robert Frost's "The Road Not Taken."

I like to read novels. My favorites are science fiction. If I had to pick one favorite, I would choose *A Wrinkle in Time* by Madeleine L' Engle.

4.15 Kyra stood on the top of the mountain. She looked down the ski slope. Breakneck Trail disappeared in the distance. She took a deep breath to steady herself.

"Don't be afraid," said Mia, her big sister. "You can make it down."

"I'm not worried about making it down," said Kyra. She forced a smile. "I'm worried about how many pieces I'll be in."

Mia patted her on the shoulder. "You don't have to do this," she said.

"Yes, I do," said Kyra. "This is the only trail on this mountain I've never gone down."

Mia smiled. "Keep your knees bent," she said, "and remember to lean into the turns."

"Wish me luck," Kyra said. She pushed off with her poles and started down the trail.

As she picked up speed, she heard Mia's voice behind her.

"Good luck."

4.16 What causes sound? The sounds of a crying baby, the slamming of a door, or the roar of a jet's engines are all produced in the same way.

Sound is caused by vibrations. When something vibrates, it moves back and forth rapidly. Imagine pulling a string on a guitar. As the string vibrates, it makes a sound.

Vibrating objects cause the molecules in the air around them to move. As the molecules move, the vibrations travel through the air in waves. When these waves reach your ear, you hear the sound.

As sound waves move away from a vibrating object, they become weaker. A sound becomes fainter the farther away you are from its source.

4.17 Have you ever played checkers? If you have, you have played one of the world's oldest games.

Games similar to checkers were played by the ancient Egyptians about thirty-five hundred years ago. A form of the game was also played in ancient Greece. The modern form of checkers appeared about five hundred years ago.

Checkers is a game of skill. Two players play against each other. Each player has twelve playing pieces on a board that has sixty-four squares. The goal of the game is to capture an opponent's pieces. The best players think ahead and take advantage of their opponent's mistakes.

Checkers is played around the world. Minor rules vary somewhat from country to country, but the basic game is the same.

4.18 Most accidents happen at home. Although nobody can prevent every accident, you can prevent many accidents by being careful and using common sense.

Many accidents occur in the kitchen. Always be careful around a stove so that you don't get burned. Don't leave paper towels, napkins, or cloths near the stove. Handle knives with care. Don't touch their sharp blades, and always cut away from your body. Keep knives in a safe place where young children can't get them.

Many accidents also occur in the bathroom. Never use electrical appliances such as a hair dryer near water. Use a rubber mat to prevent anyone from slipping in the bathtub. Keeping soap in a soap dish will help prevent people from slipping on it.

Accidents can happen to anyone. But using common sense and being careful can reduce the chances of an accident happening to you.

4.19 Hallie took her seat in the boat. She was not pleased. Her parents and she were spending one of their vacation days looking for whales. Her mom called it whale-watching. Hallie would have liked to spend the day at the lake, where her parents had rented a cabin for the week.

"This will be exciting," Hallie's mother said.

"I'd rather be swimming at the lake," Hallie said.

"You can swim every day for the rest of the week," said her father. "But you can't see a whale every day."

Hallie didn't understand what could be so great about seeing a whale. She pulled up the hood of her sweatshirt to block the cool breeze.

It was early afternoon when one of the boat's crewmen pointed ahead.

"There!" he cried.

Hallie turned and saw a fantastic creature rise from the water.

"It's beautiful," she said, and she forgot all about swimming.

4.20 Colors make the world a brighter place. Imagine how dull the world would be without colors.

Colors can be divided into three kinds: primary, secondary, and intermediate.

The primary colors are red, yellow, and blue. These are known as the basic colors. They can't be made by mixing any other colors.

The secondary colors are orange, green, and violet. Secondary colors are made by mixing two primary colors. Mixing red and yellow makes orange. Mixing yellow and blue makes green. Mixing blue and red makes violet.

Intermediate colors are made by mixing primary and secondary colors. Mixing white or black with colors will make them lighter or darker.

It is remarkable that all colors are based on combinations of red, yellow, and blue. What a colorful world the Earth is!

4.21 I was doing my homework when Annie, my little sister, came running into my room.

"Cassie, come quick!" she cried.

"What's wrong?" I said.

"It's Sasha!" Annie said between sobs. "She's stuck in a big tree." Sasha was our cat.

I followed her downstairs and out the front door.

I looked up at the big oak tree in our yard. Sure enough, Sasha was sitting on a high branch. Although she had climbed up, she was afraid to climb down.

"Sasha, come down," I said. But all I received was a sad meow.

There wasn't anything I could do except to keep calling Sasha to come down. But the cat wouldn't budge.

Fortunately, my father and mother soon came home from work. My father got the ladder from the garage and got Sasha.

I smiled as Annie scolded the silly cat.

"Sasha, don't ever do that again," she said.

4.22 When sunlight strikes water droplets in the air, a rainbow may form. The rainbow makes an arc in the sky. Sometimes its ends seem to touch the Earth.

Why does a rainbow appear when sunlight hits water droplets? The answer lies in sunlight. A ray of sunlight contains all the colors of the spectrum: red, orange, yellow, green, blue, and violet. Tiny water droplets separate the sunlight into its different colors. Under the right conditions, that creates a rainbow.

Rainbows most often are seen near the end of a rain shower. But they can also be seen in the spray of a waterfall, a fountain, or a garden hose.

According to legend, a pot of gold is at the end of a rainbow. Of course, no one can ever reach the end of a rainbow. As you approach a rainbow, it seems to move farther away and soon disappears.

4.23 Lateesha rang the doorbell to the home of Mr. and Mrs. Morgan. This was the first time she was to babysit for their son Nathan. She hoped Nathan, who was only five years old, would behave. Her friend Christina had babysat for Nathan once, and she would never do it again.

Mrs. Morgan opened the door with a big smile.

Lateesha saw Nathan standing in the living room. He was smiling too. He seemed like a nice boy.

After Mrs. Morgan gave Lateesha instructions, she and her husband got ready to leave.

"Remember, Lateesha," Mrs. Morgan said at the door, "Nathan must be in bed by nine."

"I won't forget," Lateesha said.

For the next two hours she read to Nathan, they colored, and they watched TV. Nathan was so delightful that Lateesha began to wonder if Christina had babysat for the same boy.

At nine o'clock Lateesha announced that it was time for bed.

Nathan looked at her and smiled.

"No!" he said. The firmness in his voice told Lateesha that it was going to be a long night.

4.24 It was tennis day at summer camp. Darci was to play Lora in the championship match.

Darci looked at Lora and frowned. She doubted that she could beat Lora.

"Lora's a great player," Darci said to Melissa, her best friend.

"She is," said Melissa, "but she loses her cool. She tries to hit the ball as hard as she can every time. She hits a lot of balls out of bounds. Then she gets mad and hits them even harder. That makes her miss more."

"But how does that help me?" said Darci. "I'll be lucky to return half of her shots."

"You have to play a steady game," said Melissa. "Don't make mistakes. That's how you're going to beat her."

"You mean she'll beat herself," said Darci.

Melissa nodded.

Not long after the match began, Darci knew her friend was right. When the match was finished, Darci was the tennis champ.

4.25 Captain Danos watched the main viewing screen on the bridge of his spaceship. The tiny world grew on the screen. As it became larger, oceans and land masses appeared through patchy white clouds.

"It looks much like home," said Danos to Lieutenant Tarka.

"Yes, it does," Tarka said.

"Does the planet have intelligent life?" Danos asked.

Tarka checked some instruments.

"I think it does," he said. "I'm picking up radio transmissions."

"Are the inhabitants advanced enough for us to make contact?" said Danos.

"Doubtful," Tarka said. "They seem primitive and warlike."

"Too bad," said Danos. "What's the name of the planet?"

"Earth," said Tarka.

Captain Danos gave the order to pass by Earth.